Buon Giorno, Arezzo

Buon Giorno, Arezzo

A POSTCARD FROM TUSCANY

Edited by
Suzette R. Grillot & Zach P. Messitte

Photographs by
Jacque Sexton Braun

University of Oklahoma Press : Norman

Library of Congress Cataloging-in-Publication Data
Names: Grillot, Suzette R. | Messitte, Zach P., 1968–
Title: Buon giorno, Arezzo : a postcard from Tuscany /
edited by Suzette R. Grillot and Zach P. Messitte.
Description: Norman : University of Oklahoma Press, 2016. | Includes index.
Identifiers: LCCN 2015039593 | ISBN 978-0-8061-5280-6 (paperback : alkaline paper)
Subjects: LCSH: Arezzo (Italy)—History. | Arezzo (Italy)—Description and travel. | Arezzo (Italy)—Intellectual life. | Arezzo (Italy)—Social life and customs. | Italian language—Social aspects—Italy—Arezzo. | Architecture—Italy—Arezzo. | Art, Italian—Italy—Arezzo. | BISAC: TRAVEL / Europe / Italy. | HISTORY / Europe / Italy.
Classification: LCC DG975.A7 B86 2016 | DDC 945/.59—dc23
LC record available at http://lccn.loc.gov/2015039593

Design and composition by Chris Crochetière, BW&A Books, Inc.
Manufactured in Canada.

The paper in this book meets the guidelines for permanence and durability of the Committee on Production Guidelines for Book Longevity of the Council on Library Resources, Inc. ∞

1 2 3 4 5 6 7 8 9 10

Contents

Foreword

David L. Boren

President of the University of Oklahoma

For many years, we have known that global awareness and engagement are critical for success in the global workplace. International experiences and exposure provide professional and personal benefits, which are beyond measure. Undoubtedly, the knowledge and skills that result from studying abroad enhance one's ability to compete for employment and achieve success in any chosen career. However, the benefits of an international education are even greater. Study abroad experiences enhance the development of personal characteristics and increase interest in community engagement more than any other activity. Those who study abroad are more curious, empathetic, open-minded, and humble. They are more likely to engage in civil discourse, persevere under adversity, and express gratitude toward others. American students who study abroad also see their own country with a new set of eyes and with new perspectives. These are the very qualities that characterize successful individuals and societies. The value added from study abroad experiences, therefore, cannot be overstated.

As President of the University of Oklahoma, I set out to enhance international educational opportunities for all OU students. When I took office in 1994, less than 2 percent of OU students were studying abroad. We are now sending nearly 30 percent of OU undergraduates overseas prior to graduation. With a focus on overcoming financial and academic challenges to study abroad, we are well on our way to achieving our goal of 50 percent prior to 2020. OU in Arezzo (OUA) has been the centerpiece of our international efforts and is the primary reason why we have been able to enhance global opportunities for OU students. Moreover, the creation of the College of International Studies, the hiring of dozens of internationally oriented faculty, and the annual recruitment of hundreds of international students at the University of Oklahoma have resulted in a global campus that highlights the importance of international education and awareness.

Such efforts are necessary indeed. Today's global community requires collective action. All of the issues, challenges, and problems we face around the world necessitate cooperation and collaboration. Solutions are not to be found unilaterally in isolation, but will be the result of partnerships—and to establish these partnerships, we must be globally aware and knowledgeable. Partnerships inherently require understanding. We must, therefore, study and experience the histories, cultures, politics, economics, languages, and societies of others. Our future depends on it.

(*facing*) San Domenico Church Bell Tower.

I am very pleased that this volume and our efforts in Italy and elsewhere around the world are contributing to global understanding. We are grateful to have wonderful colleagues in Arezzo and we look forward to many years of partnership between our universities, cities, and countries. In this way, the University of Oklahoma is contributing what it can to enhance greater relations within the global community.

Giuseppe Fanfani

Mayor of Arezzo, Italy, 2006–2014

On behalf of the city of Arezzo, I would like to thank the University of Oklahoma for choosing Arezzo as the location for the OU Study Center in Italy. In addition, I would like to thank the city of Norman, Oklahoma, for becoming our Sister City—a form of legal and social agreements between towns and cities.

Italy is home to many beautiful and unique places. Its uniqueness originates from a number of different factors. Arezzo is a safe, mid-sized city with strong university traditions. Moreover, Arezzo has an important and ancient history populated over the millennia with men and women who are known for their kindness, openness, and intellectual curiosity.

Many of Arezzo's most famous citizens—such as Francesco Petrarca, a scholar and poet of Renaissance Italy; Francesco Redi, a physician and poet; and Giorgio Vasari, a painter, writer, architect, and historian—represent a history of our city's determined efforts at intellectual development, economic growth, and a willingness to constantly imagine a new and better future. Today, Arezzo has one of the highest rates of entrepreneurship in Italy. This dynamism is due in part to Arezzo's commercial links with the United States and Europe. I hope that all these qualities will contribute to making the experience of international students and faculty, and tourists and visitors from around the world, more enjoyable.

I would like to express what the presence of the University of Oklahoma means for Arezzo. The University of Oklahoma students and faculty are an extraordinary portal to the world at large, a stimulus to those who grew up and live in Arezzo to be more curious and to appreciate the history of others, as well as our own history. The University of Oklahoma fits perfectly into our city and the community of Arezzo. It is an essential part of the social and cultural context of twenty-first-century Arezzo. The University of Oklahoma has been an important part of many academic, social, and cultural initiatives, many of which deserve mention, such as the Big Event, OUA Friends, and the OUA Film Festival, just to name a few. However, I would particularly like to applaud OU in Arezzo's participation in the events related to the seventieth anniversary of the Liberation of Arezzo.

Again, on behalf of the city, I thank you, not only for your choice of Arezzo, but mainly for the way and the style with which you choose to live in this city. My thank you is combined with a wish: the wish that this relationship will become stronger and more intense in the coming future—for our mutual benefit.

Cindy Rosenthal

Mayor of Norman, Oklahoma, 2007–

In May 2009, the city of Norman, Oklahoma, signed a Sister City agreement with Arezzo, Italy, in an effort to create and strengthen bonds of friendship, cultural understanding, and economic partnerships between our two communities. In large part, the relationship between our two cities grows out of a common commitment to education fostered by the University of Oklahoma's presence in Arezzo. The OU program in Arezzo has provided opportunities to hundreds of students and faculty who have been able to enjoy the history and culture of this wonderful city while living and learning at the University of Oklahoma's Study Center.

Founded in 1956 by President Dwight D. Eisenhower, Sister Cities International (SCI) is the national, nonprofit, volunteer membership organization that promotes citizen diplomacy in the United States. Sister City relationships start with people from the bottom up, and then become ratified by governments. The Sister City program strives to increase global cooperation at the municipal level, to promote cultural understanding, and to stimulate economic development by motivating and empowering private citizens, municipal officials, and business leaders to build programs of mutual benefit. In addition to Arezzo, Norman benefits from its ties with partner communities in Seika, Japan; Clermont-Ferrand, France; and Colima, Mexico.

Locally, an organization of Norman citizens —PASSPORTS—serves as host to official international visitors and exchanges. We have exchanged children's art exhibits, photos of community beautification projects, and educational and cultural visits. Many Norman citizens and OU students have had the opportunity to learn through this special city-to-city relationship, and now so can you.

This volume can only bring the two communities of Arezzo and Norman closer together. I know that many more people will have the opportunity to learn about Arezzo's treasures through the exquisite photography and rich narrative in this book. In our global neighborhood we grow closer together through the places of beauty, the treasures of art and culture, and the ties of commerce and trade. You too can explore the Etruscan remains on Poggio del Sole (aptly named "Hill of the Sun"), wind through the narrow streets and alleyways of Arezzo, discover the Piazza Grande—the most noteworthy medieval square and site of the annual Giostra del Saracino (Joust of the Saracen)—visit the many nearby hamlets within the region of Tuscany, and marvel at the splendid frescoes of the church of San Francesco. On every page, you will have the joy of discovering the special community of Arezzo.

Acknowledgments

Book projects of this scope are a cooperative effort, and many people are responsible for the outcome. We owe a debt of gratitude to the University of Oklahoma (OU) Press and in particular Byron Price, Charles Rankin, Jay Dew, and Emmy Ezzell. We thank the anonymous reviewers who provided important feedback on the manuscript, allowing us to significantly improve its content, as well as Jaci Gandenberger and Kerri Shadid for their assistance with research and editing. The photography in the book is due to the imaginative eyes of Jacque Sexton Braun. We thank all of our colleagues, the authors of the chapters, who have generously contributed their work to the book.

Beyond the book is the mutually beneficial relationship that has developed over the past ten years between OU and the city of Arezzo. When the project began, only a handful of OU students were studying abroad in Arezzo. A decade later, that number has multiplied beyond all expectations, with more than four hundred OU students now taking courses in Italy each year. The 2016 opening of the permanent OUA Study Center in Italy cements the relationship between Norman and Arezzo for years to come. Many of the authors in this book share the distinction of having been present at the creation of the special relationship between Arezzo and the University of Oklahoma. Kirk and Charlotte Duclaux deserve distinct recognition for devoting their professional careers to making OU in Arezzo a reality. And a special thank you to the hard-working staff at OU in Arezzo: Marta Agnelli, Lucio Bianchi, Patrizia Ghezzi, Beatrice Mazzi, and Flory Petcu, among others who have been involved over the years.

There are dozens of current and former faculty and staff at OU who also should take a bow for opening the pipeline between Arezzo and Norman: Millie Audas, Nicole Bisby, Serafina Boggs, Ana Bolino, Diane Brittingham, Patsy Broadway, Bridgitte Castorino, Donna Cline, Bob Cox, Merla Davis, Kaydee Dyer, Karen Elmore, Ola Fincke, Bill Forrester, Anil Gollihalli, Rob and Ellen Griswold, Tripp Hall, Nick Hathaway, Wade Hensley, Jack Hobson, Brian Holderread, Stephanie Hom, Jason Houston, Nancy Johnson, Charlie Kenney, Alice Kloker, Chris Kuwitzky, Kate Leary, Lauren Lee-Lewis, Cari Marchand, Theresa Marks, Mike Moorman, Kurt Ockershauser, Allison Palmer, Guy Patton, Leanna Payton, Cindy Rosenthal, Kristian Savic, Monica Sharp, Jim Sluss, Mitchell Smith, Fred Stritz, Clarke Stroud, the numerous members of the OU Italy Faculty Committee, the members of the OU Board of Regents, and the members of the OU Foundation.

In addition, there are members of the OU College of International Studies Board of Visitors (BOV) and other generous individuals and organizations that have supported this project. We are very grateful for the generosity of Sandra J. Cook; Molly and Jim Crawley; Mary Frates; Inasmuch Foundation; Manhattan Construction Company; Curtis Mewbourne, Jean and Kenneth Kugler, Joffa and William G. Kerr, Kavar Kerr, and the Robert S. and Grayce B. Kerr Foundation; Kay and Clark Musser; Gayle and Bill Z. Parker; Kathleen and Francis Rooney and the Francis and Kathleen Rooney Foundation; Jim Sluss; Dee Dee and Jon Stuart, Susan Peterson, and the Stuart Family Foundation; and Kathy Taylor, Bill Lobeck, Elizabeth Frame Ellison, and the Lobeck Taylor Family Foundation.

In Arezzo, there are also dozens of people who deserve our thanks: Gian Franco Borio, Emiliano Cecchini, Francesco Checcacci, Filippo Donati, Massimo Donati, Giuseppe Fanfani, Stefano Gasperini, Alessandro Ghinelli, Fabio Poggi, Paola Refrice, Gianni Rossi, Federico Siniscalco, Nick Tedford, Ginevra Villi, and Erika Zappalorti, as well as Heather Dahlstrom for all of the American baked goods she has provided to OU students in Arezzo over the years, and the many families, friends, and individuals in the community who have welcomed and nurtured OU students during their time in Italy.

Several Italian and American officials have also helped us with the creation and maintenance of OU in Arezzo. We thank Italian Ambassador Claudio Bisogniero; the Italian Consul General in Houston, Texas, Elena Sgarbi, and her predecessor, Consul General Fabrizio Nava, as well as Paolo Poli at the U.S. Consulate in Florence; and all of their colleagues in Italy and the United States for their support and assistance.

Developing a project like OU in Arezzo ultimately takes leadership—and for that we have OU President David L. Boren and First Lady Molly Shi Boren to thank. President Boren intuitively understood from the beginning that Arezzo was an ideal place for OU undergraduates to have their first glimpse of the world beyond the United States. Even more impressive, President Boren committed to developing Arezzo as a signature study abroad destination at a time when most American colleges and universities were cutting back on their overseas academic programs and when conventional wisdom questioned the value of liberal arts–study abroad programs. Bucking the prevailing winds took more than just leadership. It took courage. Luckily for all of us—President Boren has plenty of both.

The OU in Arezzo project also took vision, not only for how it would impact OU's international reputation, but for how it would blend OU's rich heritage with an Italian culture steeped in its own traditions and history. Thankfully, OU's First Lady Molly Shi Boren has that unique ability to create a communal ethos through aesthetics. Her knowledge and keen eye for gardens, art, and architecture touched this project in so many ways and allowed us to bring a little bit of Oklahoma to the valleys of Tuscany. Her vision for this project will inspire OU students and Italians alike for many generations to come. We are deeply grateful for her commitment.

Finally, we must thank the thousand-plus University of Oklahoma students who have studied abroad at OU in Arezzo for their interest in and promotion of this incredible project. This entire effort is for them, and we hope they will fondly remember for the rest of their lives their time living and learning in Italy.

—Suzette R. Grillot and Zach P. Messitte

Buon Giorno, Arezzo

Arezzo's Duomo overlooks the city.

Arezzo! An Introduction

Zach P. Messitte & Suzette R. Grillot

Arezzo is a city that few tourists or foreign students encounter on their first (or even second) visit to Italy. In fact, many tourists have never heard of Arezzo. Grand tours of the Italian peninsula make time for Rome, Florence, the Amalfi coast, Venice, and maybe Siena, but Arezzo is left happily undisturbed to go about its business as a spectacular medieval Etruscan city of about 100,000 residents with a vibrant and modern economy. Arezzo is located in the eastern part of Tuscany, not far from Umbria and the Marches, but just far enough away from the Mediterranean beaches and Alpine skiing to be safe from the elephantine tour buses that make a circus of the narrow streets of many Italian towns.

Arezzo is a *real* Italian city—a lively and livable place, not just a museum to be seen, a photo to be posted on Facebook, or a box to be checked off on a been-there-done-that list. It is, rather, a place to settle in, unpack, and take your time trying to understand what daily life under the Tuscan sun might actually be like—and perhaps dream about lingering a little bit longer. The authors and photographers who have contributed to this book fall into that category: Americans, Europeans, expatriates, Italians from other regions, students, and scholars—all who have been fortunate enough to spend considerable time in Arezzo and to be touched by its magic.

The first arrival in Arezzo matters greatly because it determines the initial glimpse into this new world. Is it mid-morning in the dead of winter at the end of a bleary-eyed overnight flight? Was the Autostrada A1 traveled

The orange terracotta rooftops of Arezzo.

through verdant springtime valleys and picturesque hilltop towns from the north (Florence) or the south (Rome)? Perhaps, instead, it is dusk in the autumn after a short ride on a fast regional train (*regionale veloce*) from Orvieto. Maybe it is the heart of summer with leafy green trees hanging over Arezzo's parks, looking out over the Casentino hills. No matter the method or season of arrival, Arezzo, like many small Italian towns tucked away from the stare of tourism, is a welcome sight.

On first arrival, Arezzo looks like an enchanted village at any time of year, appearing almost fairy-tale-like on the Tuscan highlands. The beauty comes fast along the Via Guido Monaco into town. Two thousand years of history and world-class art greet the senses at every turn, with charming piazzas, immaculate churches, stunning postcard views of the countryside, terracotta orange rooftops, exquisite restaurants, local food and wine shops, and little surprises stashed into small and winding corners of streets with ivy-covered ancient walls.

Naturally, there is more to Arezzo than first meets the eye. Appreciation for this city grows from experiencing its history, art, culture, and daily life on a regular basis. This book, with its photos and short essays, aspires to capture what makes Arezzo so unique. Foreign (and particularly American) authors, poets, artists, photographers, and filmmakers have long been captivated by Italianità (the Italian spirit or essence). Through

An abundance of fresh flowers and produce are available at the Saturday market.

Arezzo is located in Tuscany, in the center of Italy. The historical center of the city is on a hill with commanding views of the valley.

the years, visitors, including authors Henry James and Nathaniel Hawthorne; painters Mary Cassatt and James McNeill Whistler; and, more recently, film actor George Clooney and director Woody Allen have experienced the advantage of looking at the country with a foreigner's fresh eyes. Italians may have had the great fortune of being born in an enchanted land, but familiarity blinds them, in some respects, to truly seeing where they live.

The United States has long had a special relationship with Italy. More young Americans study abroad in Italy than in any other non-English speaking country. American tourists visit Italy in ever increasing numbers. American GIs fought to help liberate Italy from the Nazis (and the Italian Fascists) in the 1940s, and the United States still has more than half a dozen military bases with thousands of soldiers stationed around the country. In fact, Italians—often known for their ethnocentrism, parochialism, and somewhat unwelcoming attitude toward outsiders—are quite happy to host Americans in their towns and cities specifically because they understand the price U.S. soldiers and citizens paid to free their country during the Second World War. Visible reminders of this liberation remain, with large cemeteries for Allied troops in the south near Monte Cassino, outside Rome near the beach at Anzio where the Allies landed, and in Tuscany near Florence. Italians regularly note that they have not forgotten what America and other Allied countries did to rescue Italy from the Nazis and Fascists.

The success of Italian-Americans who came to the United States in the first part of the twentieth century also adds to the good feelings between the two peoples. The Italian-American assimilation into the United States is one of the great success stories in the history of immigration. Italian culture, from soccer to film to the Fiat 500, is popular throughout the world. Italian food (or at least the version of pizza, pasta, and *tiramisu* eaten at Italian restaurants in the United States) is a staple of modern international cuisine. The Italian coffee vocabulary (*cappuccino, macchiato, espresso, latte, venti*) is now used by anyone who regularly places an order at Starbucks. Italian wines (above all Chianti, with sparkling *prosecco* closing in fast), cheeses (parmigiano and mozzarella), and brand-name fashion (Prada, Gucci, Luxottica) are part of the global lifestyle. Things Italian are indeed familiar and comforting, which makes Italy seem a lot less foreign to visitors from abroad.

Arezzo—like most Italian cities—is its own little country within a country. Each quaint Italian town has its own unique landscape, specialized foods, and cultural practices. Arezzo is no exception, and is worthy of closer inspection. Despite the city's rich history, background, and culture, there are few volumes, if any, that examine Arezzo's past, present, and future. The city of Arezzo hosts a number of visitors and guests, such as the contributors to this book, for extended periods of time. These scholars and teachers have brought their own unique perspectives to this book with short essays about different political, cultural, and historical elements of a quintessential Italian town that has captivated each author in its own way. For students and other casual visitors who traverse the cobblestoned streets of Arezzo, this book provides a unique opportunity to learn more about a city that has so much to offer—gifts that might otherwise go unnoticed.

The book begins by providing the historical context necessary to understand the city and those who live there. Because Italians are creatures of their cities, we examine what it means to be Tuscan and Aretine as opposed to Tuscan and Sienese or Florentine. These are important distinctions, considering that authors have tried to describe the unique nature of Arezzo and the surrounding area for centuries. Understanding the layered nature of Italian history is an integral part of getting to know Arezzo. Continuously occupied since pre-Roman times—for more than two thousand years—the city is quite literally built in strata. Historical and architectural influences—Etruscan, Roman, Renaissance, Catholic, Fascist, and post–World War II—sit atop each other, brick and mortar on stone.

This first section also examines Arezzo's rich art history and architecture with a focus on the great early Renaissance painter Piero della Francesca, whose master work hangs in the Chiesa di San Francesco. As you walk through the historic center, red, yellow, and orange adorn every building, which part to reveal panoramic vistas and the twelfth-century Santa Maria della Pieve as you ascend the Corso. Around the corner is the stunning Piazza Grande with its Vasari Loggia that doubles as a grandstand during the La Giostra del Saracino in June and September.

The first section of the book concludes with a discussion of modern-day Arezzo in a chapter on post–World War II history and politics. Even seven decades after the end of the war, the scars left by Mussolini, Fascism, and the retreating Nazi Army are still visible physically (and politically) on Italy and Arezzo. Some of the fiercest fighting took place in Tuscany as the Allies advanced toward the famous Gothic Line just north of Florence in 1944 and 1945. Blocks of Arezzo (particularly near the train station) were destroyed or

The Piazza Grande is a large medieval square in the old city of Arezzo that hosts a monthly antique fair as well as La Giostra del Saracino (Joust of the Saracen) in September and June.

badly damaged during World War II and later rebuilt. Arezzo, like Tuscany, has been a solid part of Italy's *cintura rossa* (red belt), usually voting for the now defunct PCI or Communist Party (at least in the plurality) before 1989, and for the center-left since the fall of the Berlin Wall. Some interesting twists along the way include the arrest of one of Arezzo's most infamous residents, Licio Gelli, a right-wing conspirator at the heart of one of Italy's most sensational political scandals.

This book's second section explores Arezzo's linguistic distinctiveness, as well as the issues that influence daily life in Arezzo, such as its sense of identity, business environment, and status as a destination and thoroughfare for immigrants. Not unlike Arezzo's history, art, and architecture, Aretine speech patterns and accents were influenced by the Etruscans. Due to the shape of Italy's long north-south peninsula and its city-state past, distinct dialects still exist. Even in the common "high" Italian, distinct accents are detectable. This is certainly the case in Arezzo, the birthplace of one of the godfathers of the Italian language, Francesco Petrarca. While the advent of television in the 1950s may have led to less evident local accents, the Tuscan (and Aretine) way of speaking Italian remains unique (and perhaps more purely Italian) than a Sicilian, Roman, or Milanese accent. Arezzo is, as Jason Houston describes in his chapter, close to being at "the center of the Italian language universe."

Italy's modern economy and business landscape have also shaped Arezzo. While Italians have long left their home country to seek more

Walking is the preferred method of travel as automobiles are restricted inside the walls of the historic city center.

Tuscanative, a specialty shope on the Via de' Redi, offers bike tours and a sample of Tuscan food and wine.

profitable livelihoods across the ocean (notably in the United States, Canada, and Argentina), as well as in the wealthier European countries to the north (Switzerland, Germany, and the United Kingdom), Italy has more recently become a destination for Eastern Europeans, North Africans, and Chinese seeking a better life. Arezzo plays a part in Italy's twenty-first-century tides of immigration and emigration. Despite endemic economic troubles (slow growth, limited foreign investment, and the relative difficulty of starting a new business), Arezzo and the surrounding areas are full of successful small industries. "Entrepreneurship the Italian Way" takes its own unique form, navigating government bureaucracy, family history, and unique personalities. Fine craftsmanship and style, not surprisingly, continue to find a way to flourish even if the national economy remains stagnant.

The third and final section of this book highlights various aspects of Arezzo's rich and vibrant culture. Italians are internationally known for their contributions to music, fashion, film, and wine. Arezzo significantly influences each of these staples of national cultural export. Wandering around the city streets, one may hear classical music wafting from an open window or bump into a sign identifying the birthplace and home of Guido Monaco, a native son who invented the musical staff notation and started a long musical tradition that lives on in Arezzo today. Italy has become virtually synonymous with fashion and style, and the Italian "look" has become part of mainstream global culture. Arezzo-based brands, especially gold jewelry, are world famous. It is wine, however, that so many at distant restaurants and dinner tables around the world associate with Tuscany. Arezzo and its environs are home to spectacular family vineyards and hearty grapes. Arezzo's wines are unique, particularly the Chianti from the Colli Aretini, the hills around Arezzo.

Many a foreigner's first images of Italy come from film. After World War II, the Italian neorealism movement (led by directors such as Fellini, Visconti, and De Sica) pioneered a film style that accentuated real life on the silver screen. Italian actors and actresses such as Marcello Mastroianni, Claudia Cardinale, and Gina Lollobrigida became glamorous international stars. Arezzo is perhaps best known for the 1998 film *Life Is Beautiful.* Starring Roberto Benigni, it tells the poignant story of a Jewish family's travails during World War II. The film won three Academy Awards, including Best Foreign Film and Best Actor for Benigni, who, in his excitement, famously climbed over the seats of the Los Angeles glitterati to give the Oscar presenter, and fellow Italian screen star, Sophia Loren a sloppy kiss. Benigni is something of a native himself; he was born in nearby Castiglion Fiorentino, about twenty-five minutes from Arezzo.

Arezzo also brings the city's cultural past to life with a reenactment of its medieval joust twice a year. La Giostra is Arezzo's great sporting event, full of the color and pageantry of the Middle Ages. The Arezzo neighborhoods compete fiercely to win the joust and the accompanying bragging rights. Citizens are happily bedecked in full colors: the green and red of Porta Crucifera, the yellow and crimson of Porta del Foro, the white and green of Porta Sant'Andrea, and the yellow and blue of Porta Santo Spirito. The joust brings the city together, and neighbors socialize boisterously. Other sports in Arezzo are also important, but the soccer team—a point of defining loyalty in many Italian towns of similar size—is mired in the minor leagues despite a rich history, including a near elevation to exulted A League status in the 1980s.

Arezzo residents enjoy *la passeggiata*, an evening stroll, on Corso Italia. (Photo by Charles Kenney)

The ivy-covered walls of Antica Osteria l'Agania,
a restaurant on Via Giuseppe Mazzini.

Without any doubt, there is much to admire about Arezzo. The impressions and views expressed in this book are largely those of outsiders who have lived, worked, taught, and studied in the city for extended periods. While we are somewhere between casual tourists and native Aretines, this book is an extended postcard, perhaps even a love letter, to a city we admire and that we hope you will fall for, too. We want you to see more than just the first impressions of a tourist and instead learn what it is like for the Aretini to go about their lives, take a late afternoon *passeggiata* on the Via del Corso, wear their neighborhood's colors to cheer on the jousters at La Giostra in June and September, and also vote for their mayor.

Each chapter explores facets of how Arezzo fits into the national Italian narrative. The photographs of Arezzo, however, will undoubtedly be what stay with you long after you have put this book back on the shelf. Arezzo is superbly photogenic: the peculiar way the light slants against the streets, the colors of the storefronts, or the pride in the expressions on the faces of its citizens. The words are mere side dishes to the real feast: the pictorial beauty of Arezzo and the richness of its daily life in every season.

Part I History

The Archaeological Museum of Arezzo is housed in the former Olivetan convent built directly over the ruins of the Roman Amphitheater.

1 The History of Premodern Arezzo

Kirk Duclaux

The vibrant history of Arezzo is inextricably connected to its magnificent natural setting in Tuscany. Surrounded by fertile valleys, large tracts of old-growth forest, and abundant water supplies, Arezzo has riches that have always been coveted by larger cities, particularly Florence. In addition, because of its strategic location along ancient trading routes, Arezzo has prospered from the constant migration of peoples, materials, and ideas as they made their way across the Italian peninsula. Inhabited for more than twenty-five hundred years, Arezzo is the perfect city to discover the multilayered strands of history that make Italy so fascinating to explore. This essay explores Arezzo's past, from the earliest times to the rise of Florentine domination in the sixteenth and seventeenth centuries, concluding with a brief examination of how Arezzo's long history intersects with the present.

The Etruscans

Arezzo's precise founders have been lost to history, and there is no exact record of when Arezzo was settled or by whom. Archaeological evidence suggests that the area in and around the modern city of Arezzo was settled around 5000 B.C.E. Beginning around the eighth century B.C.E., during a period dominated by the Etruscans, a pre-Roman civilization, Arezzo matured into an established urban hub in central Italy, or, as it was known then, Etruria. At its political zenith, Etruscan Arezzo was one of the most important of the twelve city-states that made up the Etruscan Twelve City Confederation.

(*previous spread*) An example of the Aretine Ware pottery found in the Archaeological Museum of Arezzo.

Early settlers learned the science of viniculture, or grape cultivation, the rituals of warfare, the mechanics of land reclamation and hydraulics, the art of urban planning, the honoring of gods, and excellence in metallurgy, in particular gold and bronze. Sometime around the sixth or fifth centuries B.C.E., the Etruscans built up the city of Arezzo on the highest point in the area, to keep watch over the Arno, Tiber, and Chiana river valleys below, as well as the areas from which Arezzo drew its wealth.

On what later became St. Donatus Hill, the Etruscans built their acropolis with its important temples, and from this spiritual center the rest of the city spilled down into the lower lying neighborhoods. The modern streets, Fontanella and Pellicceria, are thought to be the original ancient *cardo*, or main north-south street upon which the early city was loosely laid out, where early inhabitants carried out social, financial, and political activities.

Anthropologists describe Etruscans as highly cultured, genteel, and extravagant in their personal habits. Women dined with men, partygoers spent months preparing for an important event, and a good fashion sense was key to social mobility. Yet this materialism, according to Roman writers, ultimately contributed to the downfall of the Etruscans in the third century B.C.E. at the hands of the Roman military machine that would eventually rule over the entire Mediterranean basin and beyond.

Roman Arezzo

Roman Arezzo, or Arretium, would continue to benefit from its natural resources and its strategic location, allowing it to serve as a bulwark against invasion from the north. Arretium also manufactured iron implements and armaments for the Roman war machine, including many of the weapons for the Roman legions battling Hannibal. Ultimately, Hannibal managed to destroy the Roman army on the shores of nearby Lake Trasimeno in 217 B.C.E. during the Second Punic War.

By the second century B.C.E., Arretium was known as Arretium Fidens (Faithful Arezzo), and the inhabitants were granted full Roman citizenship in 89 B.C.E. with all the benefits that came with that status. The ancient Etruscan city evolved into a thriving Roman metropolis, soon to become the third-largest city on the peninsula, behind only Rome and Capua, the greatest of the Roman cities of the south. Arezzo's key forum was likely located near the modern Piazza Colcitrone. The hub of economic life could be found on the cardo, along present-day Via Pelliceria. The cardo ran perpendicular to the main east-west street, known as the *decumanus*, which was somewhere in the vicinity of present day Via Oberdan or Via Pescioni. At the intersection of the cardo and the decumanus sat the main ancient forum of Arretium.

The city also boasted a large second-century amphitheater that held about ten thousand spectators, home to the famous *munera*, or gladiator events. The foundations of the amphitheater are still visible today in the park, which houses Arezzo's Archaeological Museum.

In the third to first century B.C.E., Arretium became famous for its beautiful red clay pottery, known as Red Coral Ware or Aretine Ware. Scholars have identified three main areas of production within the ancient city walls, with the largest kilns located near the present site of the University of Oklahoma in Arezzo Study Center on Via San Domenico. These kilns produced pots and vases to supply both eastern and western

The Archaeological Museum of Arezzo is housed in the former Olivetan convent built directly over the ruins of the Roman Amphitheater.

markets. Artisans made the objects shiny and delicate, as if made of red coral, by pressing them into molds and burnishing them. Collectors in the ancient world highly valued the pots for their delicate relief work and fine, coral-like finish. Aretine Ware has been found as far away as India.

By the end of the second century C.E., however, Arretium began to decline in importance. A new trade route, the Via Cassia, connected Rome to Florence, cutting off Arezzo from the Empire's bustling commercial activity. As a result, Hadrian, Rome's architect-emperor, lavished his great building campaigns on Florence rather than on Arretium. In addition, the important Aretine Ware pottery market moved northward to Gaul (the present Benelux countries), causing the once vibrant Roman stronghold to decline economically.

Early Christian Arezzo

As Roman authority was being dismantled, new Christian bishops in Arezzo asserted their own unique spiritual and temporal authority. They began at the local level, meeting challenges that would ultimately enable them to take control and solidify their place in the history of the city. According to tradition, Arezzo was the first Christian settlement outside of Rome founded by

Examples of the Aretine Ware pottery in the Archaeological Museum of Arezzo.

victims of Emperor Diocletian's anti-Christian persecutions of 303 and 304 C.E. Arezzo's subsequent seventeen-hundred-year apostolic history shows an uninterrupted line of bishops that can be traced from the first bishop of Arezzo, Saint Satyrus (died ca. 300 C.E.)—whose tomb is located in the current Duomo, or cathedral—to the present-day Archbishop Riccardo Fontana, who took office in 2009. In fact, the Catholic church canonized the first eight bishops of Arezzo, and several early Arezzo Christian leaders trace their connections with Christianity all the way back to Saint Paul.

The prominence of the early Christian faith in Arezzo is in part due to its second and most famous bishop, Saint Donatus, or San Donato, now the patron saint of the city. Donato was first ordained a deacon and then, upon Bishop Satyrus's death, elevated to the rank of Bishop of Arezzo by Pope Julius I (337–352). Through prayer alone, Donato was said to have miraculously reassembled a Communion chalice shattered by pagans; astonishingly, no wine spilled out during the rest of Communion, and scores of pagans were allegedly converted. A month later, however, a local Roman prefect arrested Donato and had him decapitated sometime in the early years of the second half of the fourth century. Tradition has it that the granite column that sits inside the present cathedral, on the left-hand side aisle, is the actual column upon which Donato was beheaded. His body is enshrined in the cathedral, but his disembodied head is venerated in a beautiful silver and jewel-encrusted reliquary in La Pieve di Santa Maria Assunta on Corso Italia. By connecting San Donato to ancient Rome, early Christianity, and even local traditions, his life becomes an integral part of the larger history of Italy.

The Rise of the Aretine Bishops in the Middle Ages

With the Roman Empire in decline, early Christian leaders such as Donato began to wield more power at the local level. A new elite class of citizens—the bishops—began to accumulate the wealth and influence that had once belonged to Etruscan and then Roman elites. The poorly named "Dark Ages" were, for Arezzo, a time of relative calm and steady prosperity under strong opportunistic bishops such as Rotari (636–652) and Cunemondo (753–782). Arezzo's cathedral complex in the Pionta area flourished under the latter. In addition, Cunemondo established an important Benedictine monastery in the area known as Il Prato—the same site where the ancient Etruscan and Roman forums once wielded influence (behind the present-day cathedral). Monasteries of this period had great power, evidence of the definitive shift from the worldview of the polytheistic Romans to that of the rising monotheistic Christians. The monasteries were also highly organized and became points of spiritual and temporal power in cities where political leadership was often weak and distant from the capital cities such as Rome and Milan. Local cathedral complexes and monasteries, like those established in Arezzo under Bishop Cunemondo, became the backbone of power that the bishops wielded over all—wealthy and poor, religious and secular. At the same time, the monasteries provided spiritual enfranchisement for both the poor and the rich alike. Under one ecclesiastical roof, the bishop organized and embraced the entire socioeconomic and political spectrums of Arezzo's society.

While the ninth-century rise of the Holy Roman Empire and the military governors, or *margraves*, who ruled in the Empire's name, kept the power of the bishops in check, the power of the Aretine bishops grew with the weakening of the Holy Roman Empire over the next two centuries. Incredibly, by the eleventh century, the Arezzo bishops ruled much of central Italy though an enormous diocesan, or district, system of control, gobbling up land that the larger powers on the Italian peninsula such as the Pope in Rome and the Duchy in Milan could not readily control. The successful power politics of early bishops such as Rotari and Cunemondo helped Arezzo move toward independence from the margraves sooner than many other communes around it. By 1098, Arezzo declared itself a legal independent commune. The bishops coupled this political power with control of the cathedral complex and its ecclesiastical school, which trained many of Tuscany's young priests, including the inventor of the staff notation used in reading music, Guido Monaco. The bishops were de facto leaders in both temporal and spiritual spheres.

Between 1052 and 1200, the bishops maintained a council with representatives chosen from the city's four distinct neighborhoods. The members of the council came from a pool of powerful feudal families who owned palaces inside the walls of the city as well as vast tracts of land in the countryside that were worked by an unskilled labor force. Wealthy aristocratic families such as the Ubertini, Azzi, and Albergotti vowed allegiance and military protection to the bishop and he, in turn, protected their local power bases against the rising merchant class. The bishop of Arezzo, therefore, was, for all intents and purposes, a feudal lord and the titular leader of Arezzo—a "bishop-count."

Under the powerful bishop-counts, the city of Arezzo grew in population and territory. The landed aristocracy, or Ghibellines, as well as the new wealthy merchant class, or Guelfs, vied for power by battling in the streets of Arezzo during the first two-thirds of the thirteenth century. The city, now an effective center of financial influence and political power, witnessed terrible violence between 1200 and 1266. Evidence of this fact is found in the story of Saint Francis of Assisi, who visited Arezzo in 1217. Seeing the citizens overwhelmed by violence, he implored a brother of his order, Sylvester, to exorcise the demons that possessed the citizens of Arezzo.

Even by medieval standards, Arezzo's familial and political vendettas made for an extremely dangerous place; 40 percent of the male citizens died by the age of twenty-five due, in large part, to the violence that ruled the cityscape. During this volatile period, wealthy families built dozens of "tower homes." Rising as high as 260 feet (80 meters), the tower homes functioned as both places of safety and places of business and entertainment. Each tower was a physical representation of its family's local power, competitive vigor, and economic might, and it was sometimes connected to other towers via substantial scaffolding networks or underground tunnels, effectively creating neighborhood enclaves. These familial clans, acting as a consortium, ruled their collective neighborhoods as if they were lords of an independent city. Some neighborhoods were gated and locked in order to maintain tariffs on incoming and outgoing goods. They minted their own coins within the gates, and only certain leaders had the keys to allow inhabitants to come and go freely—a city within a city. A resident of one Arezzo neighborhood might feel out of place, even threatened, when traveling to a neighborhood across town. He or she was, after all, a foreigner or *straniero.* (In Italian, the same word is used for

Tower homes were used for both protection and showing a family's wealth. The higher the home, the richer the family. (Photo by Wade Hensley)

The bell tower was initially a tower home, as were many others in town, and later became part of the Town Hall, with public access to it. The battlements on top of this one, as well as others on the Town Hall building, were built during the Fascist period so as to evoke national pride and traditions.

"stranger" and "foreigner"). Each of these consortiums had a parish church, the gathering place for the women who would come to pray several times a day and to honor the dead who were buried inside or in front of the church. Consider the grim realities of this time: the infant mortality rate was 50 percent, and 25 percent of women died in childbirth.

It was the bishop's job to reconcile the omnipresence of death with the church's mandate to bring salvation and everlasting life through the Blessed Sacraments. The strength of one's church community made life on earth bearable. The ringing bells of the parish church were integral to the local inhabitants' understanding of time and space. The bell tower, or *campanile*, became their spiritual and physical home base. In fact, allegiance to one's bell tower, or *campanilismo*, is a term used today to describe the affinity most Italians have with the neighborhood in which they were born and raised.

Between 1250 and 1390, Arezzo became much more like today's city, with Corso Italia emerging as the main business thoroughfare downtown. Yet, during this period of rapid growth and economic expansion, few of the city's regular citizens benefited. While Guelf merchants in other parts of Tuscany helped incite uprisings by the *popolo minuti*, or "little people," in Arezzo, the powerful Ghibelline bishops held popular sentiment in check. In fact, in these years the power of the bishops of Arezzo reached its zenith. The councils under bishop-counts such as Guglielmino degli Ubertini (1289) and Guido Tarlati (1328) were filled with so-called new men, or upper-class guild member merchants who had married into the local aristocracy and who operated out of the town hall, called the *Palazzo dei Priori*. At least in name, the Arezzo merchants were acknowledged as being a part of the political process.

The old allegiance to one's bell tower, known as the *campanilismo*, helps describe the strong bonds many Italians have to the neighborhood or town where they were raised.

Lacking power, the commoners found solace in new religious orders that took hold among the working-class communities of Arezzo. For example, construction on the Franciscan Order's main church, located in the city's historic center, began in 1290. More than a hundred years later, Renaissance master Piero della Francesca decorated its wall with fine frescoes. The poor in particular found the Franciscan equation of poverty with the life of Christ both comforting and inspiring.

Another religious order, the Dominicans, erected a church that still stands in Piazza San Domenico (ca. 1275), which was an important center of learning until suppressed by the Medici in the fifteenth century. The master painter Cimabue's *Arezzo Crucifix*, circa 1265, still hangs in its original location above the high altar. It exudes the typically Dominican calm confidence in the process by which Christians are afforded salvation. The city's current Duomo, or cathedral complex, is located on St. Peter's Hill and was also begun during this period, in 1278, thanks to an endowment of thirty thousand gold florins (roughly twelve million dollars today) left by Pope Gregory X, who died in Arezzo in 1276 on his way back from the reform council at Lyon, France. Under the guidance of Arezzo's Bishop Ubertini, the new cathedral became the spiritual center of the city. Pope Gregory X's tomb is located on the left-hand side of the cathedral, near the high altar, making him one of the few popes not buried in Rome.

A defining historical moment in Arezzo's history took place on June 11, 1289, again under the rule of Bishop Ubertini. After a glorious victory over the Sienese army just outside Arezzo in 1288, the Ghibelline forces were in high spirits. Ten thousand soldiers strong, the Ghibellines of Arezzo marched toward their next threat, the Guelfs of Florence, who were marauding in the Casentino area near the strategically located town of Poppi. The Arezzo forces were led by Bishop Ubertini, who, as punishment for some recent misdeeds, had been placed by town officials at the head of the Ghibelline army in the Casentino battlefield known as Campaldino. And Campaldino is where he died, along with two thousand other soldiers of the twenty thousand who fought there. It was on this same Campaldino battlefield that a young Italian poet from Florence—Dante Alighieri—also fought. The defeat at Campaldino, coupled with the death of the supreme Ghibelline leader, the Holy Roman Emperor Henry VII, near Siena in 1313, meant that Arezzo would soon fall under the shadow of the bigger and richer Guelf town of Florence, only fifty miles (eighty kilometers) away. The Battle of Campaldino, in fact, laid the foundation for Florentine dominance in Tuscany.

(*facing*) Cimabue's *Arezzo Crucifix* (ca. 1265) still hangs above the altar in the Church of San Domenico.

Arezzo's last hope for glory arrived in the form of a powerful bishop, Guido Tarlati. After its victory at Campaldino, Florence became occupied with wars against Pisa, thus allowing Bishop Tarlati to gain power without outside interference. After being named bishop in 1312, he became Lord of Arezzo in 1323, a position he held until his death four years later, solidifying the power base of the Ghibelline bishops-counts. Always the opportunist, Bishop Tarlati took advantage of the weakness of a distant papacy, now located in Avignon, to seize papal lands. No doubt the emperor encouraged this action by asking Bishop Tarlati, rather than the pope, to crown him as Holy Roman Emperor. Sadly for Tarlati, Pope John XXII excommunicated him in 1325, labeled him a heretic in 1327, and condemned him to

Beautiful frescos cover the walls of the Duomo.

death. Tarlati, a pawn in a chess game between an emperor and a pope, cheated the executioner by dying of natural causes shortly after his sentence.

In 1337, after years of losing territory and prestige, Arezzo finally became a subject state of Florence, ingloriously sold to the Florentines by the shrewd and self-serving brother of Guido Tarlati, the mercenary Pier Saccone Tarlati (d. 1365) for eighteen thousand gold florins (over seven million dollars today). The city was again sold in 1384 for a much heftier sum of forty thousand florins (sixteen million dollars today) paid to the Florentines by a mercenary from Naples as part of a Byzantine plan hatched by a member of the Tarlati family.

Arezzo under the Florentines

Dante once described the Aretines as "*botoli ringhiosi*," or growling dogs. The Aretines earned this moniker by revolting against Florence six times between 1409 and 1530. Each time the Florentines crushed a rebellion, the Aretines revolted again. Finally, in 1561 under the reign of the Florentine Duke Cosimo I, Arezzo became a truly subject

Palazzo delle Logge was designed by Giorgio Vasari in 1573.

state. Duke Cosimo's workmen effectively erased almost a third of the medieval area of the city when they destroyed its most important civic and religious buildings, most of which sat on the St. Donatus Hill behind the cathedral. In their place, Cosimo built a fortress that stands to this day, a visible reminder of the power of the Medici dukes. Cosimo eviscerated the political body of the city, as well as its spiritual heart. He razed the ancient cathedral complex of Arezzo at Pionta and used the stones of that beautiful seven-hundred-year-old cathedral to build his fortress. With the construction of the fortress, Duke Cosimo I wiped away over thirteen hundred years of Arezzo's history.

Nothing is more telling of how Arezzo had fallen behind Florence than a comparison of the populations of the two cities in the late fourteenth century. Florence developed into a bustling mercantile city-state, home to the third-largest population (about one hundred thousand) in Europe after London and Paris. By contrast, Arezzo's population had dropped to roughly four or five thousand. Much of this decline had to do with the fact that Florence prospered economically by drawing its workforce from the countryside and subject cities. Another reason for the population's flight might have been the heavy tax burden placed on the citizens of Arezzo. The local church also suffered. New taxes were levied on the diocese, which had been previously exempt. Taxing the church broke down the long-standing power of the nobles, some of whom harbored rebellious intents.

In spite of Arezzo's decline, many important intellectuals were born in and around the city during this period. Several studied at the famous cathedral schools at Pionta and San Domenico, and eventually made their way to Florence, Pisa, or Rome to pursue their fortunes. The great humanist scholar Petrarch (d. 1374); the chancellors during the Golden Age of Florence (1498–1512), Leonardo Bruni (d. 1444) and Carlo Marsuppini (d. 1453); the satirist and playwright Pietro Aretino (d. 1556), known to many as the "Scourge of Princes" because of his flair for mixing flattery with blackmail in order to secure positions at court, were all natives of Arezzo. Even the great Michelangelo (d. 1564) was born in nearby Caprese. The bibliophile and humanist Poggio Bracciolini (d. 1459) and the painter and mathematician Piero della Francesca (d. 1492) called Arezzo home for a while before moving on to larger cities. And architects such as Bernardo Rossellino, Benedetto, and Giuliano da Maiano worked in Arezzo to give the city the Renaissance feel it has today. However, the man who contributed the most to Arezzo was the prolific artist and writer Giorgio Vasari (d. 1574). Vasari built the beautiful loggia in Piazza Grande and the altarpiece in the Badia church, and transformed the interior of the cathedral into what we see today.

Arezzo continued to produce notable intellectuals in the seventeenth century during the Age of Enlightenment, when the seeds of scientific curiosity and knowledge sown in the Renaissance began to bear fruit. Andrea Cesalpino (d. 1603) conducted experiments on the nature of circulating blood in the human body. Francesco Redi (d. 1697), the eminent physician, challenged the Aristotelian notion of spontaneous generation.

Arezzo's rich twenty-five-hundred-year history is the foundation for the modern, thriving city of one hundred thousand inhabitants today. Aretines are rightfully proud of their city's contribution to the intellectual and artistic heritage of Italy. Arezzo's story, while perhaps lesser known than those of Florence or Siena, nevertheless merits its own chapter in understanding Italy's impact on the modern world.

2

Art and Art History in Arezzo

Allison Palmer

Arezzo's strong political and economic history gave rise to a sophisticated culture that has extended into the modern era. The evidence of Arezzo's rich past can be seen in the many works of art that remain in the city.

The *Chimera of Arezzo* (ca. 400 B.C.E.) is an important piece in the city's artistic history and a particularly beautiful Etruscan sculpture made of hollow-cast bronze. Attributed to an ancient Greek workshop in southern Italy, the 120-centimeter-tall sculpture depicts a vibrant female lion crouching down on her front legs while her hind legs remain tense. Her mouth is open in a fierce, fiery roar. A full mane and ears pushed forward frame her face. The rippling ribcage of the lean lion extends into a goat's head, which is attached to the side of the lion, and from her curved back flows a tail in the form of a serpent's head. The animal is wounded, as the goat's neck droops to reveal a few drops of blood. The chimera, at the moment of her death, begins to draw up in fear. It is this particular aspect of the chimera that makes the work unique. According to Greek mythology, a chimera is a fire-breathing beast created from a combination of animals—a lion's body, legs, and head; a serpent's tail; and a goat's head attached to the side of the lion's body. Originating in Asia Minor, the legendary animal was first described in Homer's *Iliad* and was considered a bad omen, particularly one of natural disasters.

The bronze casting technique of the *Chimera of Arezzo* dates to ancient Greece, where the lost-wax molding method was perfected in the sixth century B.C.E. Because of the incredible weight and expense of bronze, large works such as the *Chimera of Arezzo* are hollow casts. In this process, parts of the body are modeled

A bronze replica of the *Chimera of Arezzo* is located in the Porta San Laurentino near the spot where the original was found.

(*facing*) The original *Minerva of Arezzo* resides in the National Archaeological Museum in Florence, but a replica can be found on Via Pescioni in Arezzo.

BRE 2002
RICORDO
INAUGURAZIONE
BRONZO DELLA MINERVA
QUARTIERE DI PORTA CRUCIFERA

separately with a solid clay core, then layered with wax and covered by an outer layer of clay. The wax is then melted out to create a hollow shell into which the molten metal is poured. The clay exterior is cracked off, all parts are soldered together, and the bronze is filed and incised to a finished image. When the *Chimera of Arezzo* was dug up just outside the city walls in 1553, it was initially described as a lion, but the serpent tail was later found and reattached, and the sculpture was correctly identified as the *Chimera of Arezzo*. Shortly after its discovery, the bronze creature was taken to Florence at the request of Duke Cosimo I de' Medici, where it remains today at the National Archaeological Museum.

A few years before the Renaissance discovery of the *Chimera of Arezzo,* a bronze figure of Athena, or Minerva, was discovered in Arezzo by workmen digging a well. This figure, called the *Minerva of Arezzo,* was similarly transferred to Florence by order of the Medici and is also located in the National Archaeological Museum today. A copy of the work can be found on Via Pescioni in Arezzo. The original statue, an ancient two-meter-tall work cast around 280 B.C.E. in a Greek foundry, was missing its right arm and a portion of its back, but has been reconstructed and restored over the centuries.

Ceramic ware was also an important artistic medium in Etruscan Arezzo and suggests extensive trade with ancient Greece. A red-figure volute krater from around 510 B.C.E., attributed to the famous Greek artist Euphronios and now located in the Archaeological Museum of Arezzo, is an example of the high quality of pottery that was available in the ancient city. This large vessel, with a wide neck and scroll-shaped volute handles, was used in antiquity to mix water and wine. It was rediscovered in the 1700s, during a period of renewed interest in antiquity.

Euphronios worked at a time when black-figure vase painting was giving way to the more naturalistic and highly detailed red-figure technique characteristic of the Early Classical era. The central portion of the vessel is elaborate, depicting a battle between Heracles (the Roman-named Hercules) and his friend Telamon against a group of Amazons. The Amazons were fierce female warriors who lived in what is now Turkey, where they maintained a kingdom and came to be known as "killers of men" or "those who fight like men." While Telamon stands over a wounded Amazon dressed in Scythian clothing, Heracles avoids an arrow shot by the Amazon Teisipyle. Around the frieze of the krater are drunken revelers forming a procession, a scene often paired with stories of Heracles. The appearance of this same scene on later kraters on the Italic peninsula might suggest that the Arezzo krater was widely known. Pottery was one of the most important industries in Etruscan Arezzo and thrived under Roman Republican rule, when both Augustan pottery and coins were produced in vast quantities in Arezzo.

Arezzo flourished under Roman rule and expanded down the hill on its southern edge, where Gaius Maecenas commissioned the construction of a Roman amphitheater near the Etruscan city walls. Maecenas, a political advisor to Caesar Augustus in Rome who traced his family back to the wealthy Etruscan Cilnii of Arezzo, is best known for being a generous patron of the arts, mainly of the Augustan poets. Built at the end of the first century C.E., the oval amphitheater had two sets of stairs and seats to accommodate around eight thousand people, and was used primarily for theater performances. The complex was made from a combination of sandstone, bricks,

Bronze vase in the Archaeological Museum of Arezzo.

and marble, in a manner similar to the much larger and more famous elliptical Coliseum built in Rome about the same time and used primarily for athletic events. Only a rough semicircle of mounded stone remains of the Arezzo structure, which suffered from looting throughout the Middle Ages, when reusing ancient materials, or *spolia*, was considered an ideological and practical form of recycling. Today, the partially exposed remains of the stalls and ambulatories, or walkways, set around the oval are maintained in a park-like setting open to the public.

Detail of Cimabue's *Arezzo Crucifix*. (Photo by Charles Kenney)

Arentine art of the late medieval period is also significant in part because both the Church and the emerging ruling class began to commission works to solidify their spiritual authority and affirm their political worth. The Church used art to educate and inspire congregants; indeed, it was a powerful form of communication in this age of low literacy rates prior to the invention of the printing press in the 1400s. Similarly, civic patrons showed their status and worth to the community by having access to the expensive material goods and cultural connections needed to possess beautiful works of art. Thus, while art was elite, its communicative function required an audience, and the introduction of naturalism helped make art more visually accessible to the broader public, or *popolo*.

On the high altar of the small neighborhood Church of San Domenico in Arezzo hangs one of the earliest crucifixes in Italy to show the emerging naturalism of the late medieval Gothic era, which anticipates the Renaissance period. This large wooden painting, done in egg tempera, is attributed to Cimabue, who is likely the artist named Bencivieni di Pepo, born in Florence around 1240 and written about in both Dante Alighieri's *Divine Comedy* (ca. 1310) and Giorgio

Pietro Lorenzetti's *Madonna and Child Polyptych* painting is displayed on the high altar of the Pieve.

Vasari's *Lives of the Most Excellent Italian Painters, Sculptors, and Architects, from Cimabue to Our Times* (1550). Cimabue is credited with establishing the stylistic shift from late medieval Byzantine abstraction to naturalism. The scene of the crucifixion, so central to Catholic liturgy, emerged in the Byzantine, or Eastern, Church in the 600s, and it usually revealed an abstract figure of Christ, flattened and rendered in geometric form, with eyes open and staring forward in the eternal gaze of victory over death. In Cimabue's work, dated around 1265 when Cimabue was working in Arezzo, a new *pathos* emerged. Cimabue depicted Christ with his head slumped toward the end panel of his mother, eyes closed, blood dripping from his wounds, and stylized muscles shown in painful tension. The Passion Cycle assumed greater importance in the Catholic Church beginning in the late 1100s, and end panels were sometimes added to explain the history of these Crucifixion scenes. Cimabue's *Arezzo Crucifix* shows the Virgin Mary and John the Evangelist in these panels. The grief-stricken figures increase the emotion, and thus the humanity, of the work. Such thematic and stylistic changes coincided with the addition of several new mendicant, or begging, orders, including the Dominicans in the 1200s. The Dominican Order, approved in 1216, provided a new spiritual outlet for people in burgeoning cities such as Arezzo, where preaching in the vernacular became a powerful way to evangelize directly urban populations. Cimabue's *Arezzo Crucifix* in San Domenico in Arezzo is an excellent example of the convergence of these religious and artistic changes.

Political issues also drove art production in Arezzo. Pietro Lorenzetti's painting *Madonna and Child Polyptych*, commissioned in 1320 for the high altar of the Romanesque church of Santa Maria Assunta (called the Pieve), situated on the main avenue in Arezzo, is a good example of political art. The Pieve, completed in the early thirteenth century, was built in the Romanesque style of architecture, a style best known for its use in the famous cathedrals of Lucca and Pisa, both begun in 1063.

This multi-paneled wood altarpiece, or polyptych, also done in egg tempera paint, is described as a *tabula Beate Virginis Marie* in the original commission document drawn up between Lorenzetti and his ecclesiastical sponsor, Bishop Guido Tarlati di Pietramala. The Lorenzetti polyptych is a well-preserved example of the late Gothic / Early Renaissance style, blending abstraction and naturalism in the gold-leaf background set behind the moving figures. The central section portrays the Virgin and Christ child, flanked by separate paired panels with half-length figures of Saint Donatus and John the Evangelist to the viewer's left and John the Baptist and Saint Matthew to the viewer's right. Saint Donatus is the patron saint of Arezzo, and the Pieve is dedicated to the Assumption of the Virgin Mary. Above these figures are four more paired figures that include, from left to right: the Roman martyrs John and Paul; Saints Vincent and Luke; James Major and James Intercisus; and Tuscan martyrs Marcellinus and Augustinus. These figures range from the lesser-known Saint Vincent, who maintained a cult following in nearby Cortona, and James Intercisus, who had a small following in nearby Siena, to the more famous Roman saints, including Luke, best known for painting the first image of the Virgin Mary as she appeared miraculously before him. Between these paired figures are small prophet medallions. Above the Virgin is a scene of the Annunciation flanked by Saints Reparata, Catherine, Ursula, and Agatha. The Assumption of the Virgin, *Maria Assunta*, appears alone in the uppermost middle panel. A *predella*, or painted base, is missing today. This altarpiece, the first definitively dated work of Pietro Lorenzetti, was completed about fifty years after Cimabue's *Arezzo Crucifix* and reveals a further step toward the naturalism so characteristic of the Renaissance. The painting is also a testament to both the increased importance of the ecclesiastical administration of the Pieve in Arezzo and to the communal involvement in its art patronage through donations that spanned all levels of society, allowing art to be more accessible to the *popolo*.

Greater access to visual art led to a more narrative form so that viewers could read and interpret images similar to how we read text today. Increasingly, larger narrative works also set the tone for both familial and communal aspirations. The sculpted stone wall tomb in the Cathedral of Arezzo of Guido Tarlati di Pietramala, Bishop of Arezzo (1312–27) and Lord of Arezzo (1321–27), is considered one of the most important funerary monuments of the Early Renaissance. The Cathedral, also called the Duomo, overlooking the town of Arezzo to the south and the Casentino Valley to the north, was built beginning in 1278 in the Gothic style. The wall tomb, originally located to the right of the high altar in the Tarlati family funerary chapel but now on the left, has an elevated bier that holds the sculpted reclining body of Guido Tarlati, tilted out toward the viewer below. An empty arched and curtained space above is topped by a Gothic gable and filled with a low relief image of the imperial eagle of the Holy Roman Emperor, to whom the Tarlati family remained loyal. Below the bier are four registers, or levels, with four narratives in each register, elevated onto the wall by slender piers. Fate changed quickly in late medieval Italy, and in 1341, the monument was vandalized in an uprising, and some of the scenes were destroyed. Later in the century it was restored and moved to its current location in the cathedral.

Aretines continued to patronize the arts by building family and religious memorials, even during the economic and political decline of Arezzo during the fourteenth century. Indeed, the largest and best-known art commission in Arezzo is Piero della Francesca's monumental fresco, *Legend of the True Cross*, painted in the Church of San Francesco in this period. This fresco commission was made possible by a large bequest from the Bacci, a family of merchants from Arezzo living in Florence who planned their family funerary monument back in their hometown. Arezzo was predominantly Franciscan at this time, and the Franciscan Order received about a third of all Aretine bequests. Indeed, the Church of San Francesco is the third most prominent church in Arezzo, after the Duomo and the Pieve. As noted in the previous chapter, Saint Francis of Assisi is said to have stopped outside Arezzo in 1217, and standing next to the city gates, ordered his companion, Brother Sylvester, to exorcise the demons that plagued the city. A Franciscan church was later built outside the city walls. This story is memorialized in a late-medieval fresco scene on the wall of the Upper Church of San Francesco in nearby Assisi, the hometown of Saint Francis.

Bicci di Lorenzo painted frescoes of the four Evangelists on the cross-vaulted ceiling of the chapel inside the Church of San Francesco. When Lorenzo died in 1452, Piero della Francesca was hired to paint the wall frescoes. Piero, born in the nearby Florentine town of Sansepolcro, is best known for his geometric style of painting and superior fresco technique. Piero's work covers the three walls of the chapel and narrates the story of

The Baptism of Christ (1549) by Giorgio Vasari is displayed in the Duomo Museum in Arezzo.

the *Legend of the True Cross* across three registers on each wall. The story, of special interest to the Franciscan Order, traces the provenance of the wood used to crucify Christ. Piero's narrative does not follow the Western norm of reading from left to right, top to bottom, but instead the stories are visually linked across the chapel where they are read either from right to left or across the chapel space.

The *Legend of the True Cross* story begins with the top right wall scene, viewed from the nave, which shows the *Story of Adam*, paired across the space with the ending scene of *The Exaltation of the Cross*. The middle right scene is divided into two parts to show the *Story of Sheba and Solomon*, highlighting the moment when Queen Sheba recognizes the cross, kneels down to pray, and later tells Solomon about this miracle-working piece of wood. The scene opposite shows a two-part narrative of *Helen on Her Pilgrimage to Jerusalem*, kneeling down to pray at the wood used in the crucifixion, and then proving its miracle-working powers with the resurrection scene. The bottom two wall scenes show two battles—on the viewer's left is *The Battle of Heraclius*, and on the right is the *Battle of Constantine*. The narrow scenes that flank the window behind the high altar show the *Raising of Judas from the Well* on the left and the *Burial of the Wood* on the right, which are visually linked through similar composition. The bottom two registers show the *Annunciation* on the left and the *Dream of Constantine* on the right, both of which are scenes of angelic pronouncement. Piero's fresco technique shows how tempera colors can be applied to damp plaster in order to create a stable bond as the colors seep into the plaster as it dries. However, he also applied some pigments onto dry plaster to heighten the intensity and depth of the colors.

Piero della Francesca was a subject of Giorgio Vasari's *Lives of the Most Excellent Italian Painters, Sculptors, and Architects*, first published in Florence in 1550 with a dedication to Cosimo I de' Medici, and enlarged and republished in 1568 to include woodcut illustrations. Vasari favored Tuscan artists, and his belief in the supremacy of Renaissance naturalism codified a stylistic formula still followed today. Weaving together fact and fiction, Vasari told of the lives of artists from the late Middle Ages through his own time in such a way that Tuscan Renaissance art emerged as superior across Europe. This book is the biography of the first artist written in an encyclopedic format, and is considered the first art historical text.

Vasari was also a painter, writer, architect, and humanist scholar born in Arezzo in 1511. He went to Florence to study painting at an early age, and later visited Rome. Although Vasari spent much of his life in Florence, furthering his humanist education and painting primarily for the Medici family, he maintained ties to Arezzo, designing and decorating a grand home that is now a museum, renovating several churches, and completing several paintings located throughout the city. His most famous work in Arezzo is the elegant open portico and loggia along the top of Piazza Grande in the center of the city. Begun in 1573, it mimics the general structure of the Vasari Corridor that he built ten years earlier in Florence to link together several buildings within the Medici compound. The classical design of the Arezzo portico, revived from Roman antiquity, gave the city greater cultural importance and a "modern" look, keeping up with the classicism that was sweeping across the Italian peninsula. The Vasari Corridor in Florence provided a visual symbol of Medici control of the city, and the Vasari portico in Arezzo created a visual link between Arezzo and Florence to confirm Medici political ties, while also modernizing the medieval downtown.

A good example of Vasari's own painting style is his *Baptism of Christ*, a large oil painting from 1549 located in the Duomo Museum in Arezzo. This work shows Christ on the left, with his arms across his chest, left leg straight and right leg bent, and head bowed down to receive the baptismal water. To the right is John the Baptist, wearing a light pink robe that exposes one leg and his torso while holding the water above Christ's head in an elegant, almost frozen, pose. Three angels kneel at a river that extends beyond Christ, while two *putti*, or baby angels, hover in the sky above, flanking the white dove that symbolizes the Holy Spirit.

In subsequent centuries, Arezzo would continue to maintain its important cultural heritage, helping to preserve the city's significant contribution to the history of art. The creations left behind by the artists and architects who lived in Arezzo are a treasure trove for historians seeking to understand the past as well as for art lovers from around the world. Arezzo has a special niche as one of Italy's most important cities for art.

ELISEO
BROCHEREL
PARTIGIANO COMBATTENTE
UCCISO PER MANO FAS ISTA
6 GIUGNO 1944

3

The Liberation of Arezzo

Beatrice Mazzi & Zach P. Messitte

The scars of World War II are still evident in Arezzo over seventy years after the Allied forces liberated the city from the Nazis on July 16, 1944. The passage of seven decades has also created a gap between those who personally experienced the war and the economic deprivation and hunger that followed, and those born after 1960. The wounds are physical as well as psychological. Allied bombs destroyed parts of Arezzo's neighborhoods in the historic center, including the railroad station and several central downtown buildings. As modern construction filled the empty spaces created by the war, the architectural sanctity of the medieval town was irrevocably changed. Wandering around the streets of Arezzo, one sees buildings out of place and seemingly in the wrong century. Commemorative stones, memorials, and monuments, complete with embossed names, photos, and dates, serve as a constant reminder of one of the most difficult times in Arezzo's history. These monuments do not lessen the impact of the terrible experiences of war, but their interpretation and importance have evolved with the needs of the twenty-first century. The city of Arezzo and its residents have learned to heal, cope, and move forward.

Not unlike the liberation of Italy, Arezzo's own battle was a microcosm of the country's disastrous involvement with Fascism and World War II. Benito "Il Duce" Mussolini's rise to power culminated in two decades of Fascist dictatorship that ended with his capture and public hanging in Milan in 1945. These

(*facing*) World War II memorial honoring a partisan killed by the Fascists on June 6, 1944.

twenty-one years changed Italy and Arezzo. The country's imperial adventures in Africa and the delusions of a new Roman Empire in the 1930s led to the disastrous entry into the war on the side of the Germans in 1940. Italy's war with the United States followed Pearl Harbor as Mussolini joined in solidarity with its Axis partners, Germany and Japan. The war did not go well for the Italians. Unprepared for conflict and enduring heavy casualties, Mussolini led the country into military disasters and humiliation on the battlefield. By 1943, with the Italian army in disarray and the Allied invasion of Sicily underway, the Fascist Grand Council in Rome pushed Il Duce out of power and the King of Italy signed an armistice with the Allies. Mussolini then led the short-lived Republic of Salò, named for the small town on Lake Garda in northern Italy where he held Fascist court. Arezzo and Tuscany lay beyond Allied lines, nominally falling under the new Mussolini-led Nazi puppet state until the summer of 1944.

Nazi troops arrived in Arezzo on September 13, 1943, and easily took control of the entire province. Italian political and military institutions had collapsed at the national, regional, and local levels. A new conflict emerged between the collaborationists of the Social Republic of Salò, loyal to Mussolini and Hitler, and the anti-Fascist partisans of the National Committee of Liberation. The anti-fascist citizens of Arezzo were mainly students, former prisoners of war, Communists, Socialists, and Italian Army deserters who banded together to fight Mussolini and Hitler. With meager resources at their disposal, they organized a local resistance movement that was ordered into two principal factions: the XXIII Brigade Pio Borri, named in honor of a martyred nineteen-year-old partisan, and the Brigade Bande Esterne, a group that drew its support from the people in the valleys surrounding Arezzo. Local streets, libraries, and schools still bear the names of the partisans who led the struggle: Sante Tani, Pio Borri, Licio Nencetti, Antonio Curina, Eugenio Calò, and Modesta Rossi. Along with many other ordinary men and women, these partisans courageously opposed the Fascists and risked their lives for a modern Italy.

With the advance of the Allies up the peninsula in late 1943, major urban centers and railroad hubs became the target of American and British pilots looking to disrupt German communication and troop movements. On November 14, 1943, the first bombs fell on Arezzo. The toll of the air campaign had serious consequences for the economy of the city and accounted for much of the physical damage to the town that would take years to reconstruct following the war. The Allies dropped an estimated eighteen hundred tons of bombs on Arezzo and the surrounding area. According to Antonio Curina, the city's first postwar mayor, 60 percent of the city was destroyed between late 1943 and mid-1944. Beginning in December 1943, many Aretines moved to the countryside in order to escape the bombing, finding shelter in the farms of friends or relatives or in the tunnels of the old Apennine railway line. The German command and the Italian Fascists were headquartered just outside of town at the Villa Occhini and the Villa Godiola. Today these villas are respectively a luxury resort and an international theatre academy. The local Roman Catholic Church offered some charitable support to those in need, and several local priests were sentenced to death and killed by the Nazis for their collaboration with the partisans.

The Allied liberation of Italy between 1943 and 1945 was a protracted operation, particularly in

Tuscany. More than a hundred thousand Allied and Nazi soldiers and Italian civilians were killed during the campaign as the Allies pushed slowly northward up the peninsula. Led by the British Eighth Army, the American Fifth Army under the command of General Mark Clark, and a host of Allied forces from a diverse set of countries that included Brazil, Poland, and New Zealand, they liberated Rome in June 1944. The area to the north, including Arezzo, remained under Fascist control. Hitler and his Italian campaign field marshal, Albert Kesselring, established the Gothic Line along the Apennines that would mark the Nazis' last stand before the open plains of the Po Valley. The Gothic Line ran from just south of La Spezia on the Mediterranean in the west to Pesaro on the Adriatic to the east. Located less than fifty miles south of the Gothic Line, Arezzo was a major rail hub connecting Rome to Florence, giving it significant strategic importance to the Germans and the Allied forces. The rolling hills around Arezzo also made it easier for the partisans to hide and conduct hit-and-run guerrilla warfare. On the other hand, it made it more difficult for the Allies to root out the Nazis and their Italian Fascist collaborators.

All urban services, including hospitals, newspapers, and the wartime rationing system, broke down in the winter of 1944. A shortage of food added to the desperate situation. All able-bodied local men were conscripted to boost the ranks of Mussolini's Fascist army. Many were forced to enlist or face a death sentence. The last Fascist head of Arezzo Province, Melchiore Melchiori, commanded the partisans to lay down their arms and surrender their weapons on penalty of death. The local partisans defied the order and continued to resist. By the spring of 1944, they openly disobeyed the Nazis by lighting great bonfires on the mountains surrounding the city. Citizens of small hill towns such as Poti and Pratomagno, visible from Arezzo's historic center, helped set these illegal blazes as farmers and Aretines in solidarity with the partisans spontaneously joined the demonstration against the Nazis.

The activities of the partisans intensified as the Allied forces drew closer to the city in the spring of 1944. They organized ambushes, surprise attacks, and sniper activity that hampered the ability of the Germans to maintain order. The British and American armies advanced from the south. The British liberated Lazio and Umbria from the retreating German Army and by early July had also taken towns close to Arezzo, such as Lucignano and Cortona. The people of Arezzo thought liberation was imminent as well. Local partisans descended from the hills around the city with Fascist prisoners in tow and settled outside the city, ready to help the British should they enter Arezzo. On the night of July 4, 1944, a group of partisans entered Arezzo and hid downtown in the Palazzetto Albergotti, on Via della Fioraja, with the intention of supporting the British troops from inside the city. Unfortunately, German opposition slowed down the advance of the British, who were engaged in a fierce battle on the outskirts of Arezzo. Surrounded by mountains, Arezzo proved to be a difficult city from which to dislodge German foes.

Within a few miles of Arezzo, the Germans constructed elaborate machine gun nests and trenches complete with barbed wire and anti-tank ditches. The citizens of Arezzo and nearby towns were not spared the brutality of the retreating Nazi Army.

In order to discourage the general population from helping the partisans and the Allies, the

The San Polo Memorial, located just outside Arezzo, honors the Italians murdered by the Nazis just days before the liberation of the city in July 1944.

Nazis employed particularly harsh retribution tactics. Thousands of innocent civilians (including women and children) were massacred for collaboration with the partisans or for the killing of a German soldier. Nazi troops, with the collaboration of Italian Fascist fighters, carried out indiscriminate massacres of civilians in villages near Arezzo, including the towns of Mulinaccio, Staggiano, Badicroce, Molin dei Falchi, Pietramala, and San Severo. One of the most infamous of these reprisals took place in the town of San Polo, just northeast of Arezzo, where sixty-five Italians were tortured and killed in July 1944, just days before the Allied liberation of Arezzo. The Nazis indiscriminately slaughtered the elderly, women, and children, as well as Italian partisans, including Eugenio Calò, a Jewish-Italian resistance leader from Pisa, who was posthumously awarded Italy's highest honor for heroism. In the end, more than twelve hundred civilians from Arezzo and the surrounding areas were killed during the Nazi retreat, making the city a witness to some of the worst violence in Italy during World War II. In Anghiari, near Arezzo, the Fascists also established a concentration camp for Yugoslavs, where more than ten thousand Slovenes were held in poor conditions in 1942 and 1943.

The final stages of the liberation of Arezzo began on July 13, 1944, when the British launched an attack on the hills to the south and east of the city. On the same day, a division of New Zealanders tried to break the German resistance on nearby Mount Lignano, while the Ninth Gurkha Rifle Corps conquered the summit of another peak, Mount Favalto, thanks to the work of the ex-miners of Mumbai (Bombay, India). The miners ingeniously opened up a Jacob's ladder of sorts—a secret underground pathway that allowed Allied soldiers to enter Arezzo via the Palazzo del Pero. After two days of fierce fighting, the Germans retreated on July 15, and the first British soldiers entered the city on the morning of July 16, 1944. The British took possession of Arezzo

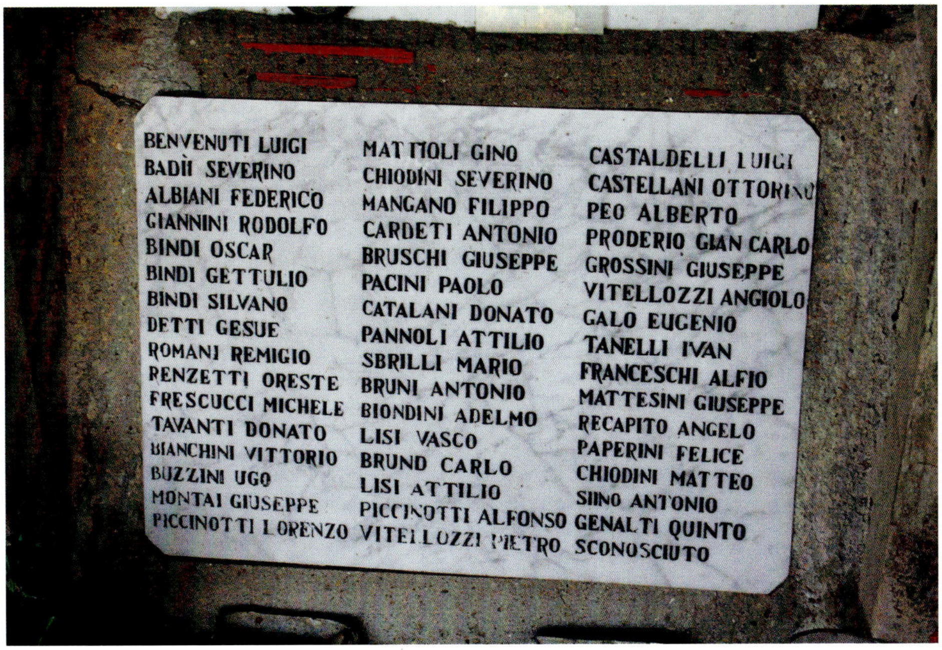

The names of the of those killed by the Nazis at San Polo include women, children, and elderly Italians as well as partisans fighting the retreating Fascists.

Farmhouse storage in San Polo where victims were killed.

San Polo Massacre memorial.

without any significant fight. One newspaper described the fall of Arezzo on July 17:

> Those of us who came to Arezzo an hour or two after our advanced troops, found it a deserted town, ghostlike in the silence that was broken only by the rumble of approaching tanks. The main street through the town from the south was a melancholy line of battered shop fronts and doorways. It looked as if one great explosion had pushed everything sideways but left the walls standing.

The wartime experiences left scars on Italy and Arezzo that linger today. Some who remember the period firsthand find fault with the partisans, arguing that their actions or strategic mistakes provoked violence as Nazi soldiers retreated north toward Germany. German military documents, however, suggest that many of the brutalities had little to do with the activities of the partisans. The Nazis in their retreat up the Italian peninsula followed a scorched-earth policy of "total war" designed to intimidate civilians, isolate the resistance movement from the rural population, and terrorize Italian communities. Nevertheless, the events of 1943–44 still divide Italian public opinion more than seventy years later, often splitting along political lines, given that many of the partisan leaders were either Communists or Socialists.

Arezzo's ancient city walls still stand—and the passerby could well ignore the echo of the rumbles of war gone by. Today's city of Arezzo is not only a showcase for Etruscan and Roman architecture or the wondrous frescoes of the early Renaissance—it is also a city that had to undergo and move past a painful page of history. The commemorative stones visible in Arezzo are scattered and sometimes neglected. They vouch, however, for a difficult period in the city's history.

(*facing*) The Mulinaccio Memorial, located just outside Arezzo, honors the fifteen Italians killed by the Nazis in July 1944.

A RICORDO PERENNE DEI 15 TRUCIDATI
DALLE ORDE TEDESCHE IN FUGA
IN QUESTO MEDESIMO LUOGO
LA SERA DEL 6 LUGLIO 1944
POSSA L'ESTREMO SACRIFICIO DI LORO
INERMI ED INNOCENTI
SEGNARE AGLI UOMINI

4

Arezzo's Modern Politics and History

Zach P. Messitte

The Lingering Effects of World War II

The period between the rise of Italian Fascism in the 1920s and Victory in Europe Day (V-E Day) in May 1945 still casts a long shadow on Italy's politics and history. Even in Arezzo, the conflict remains a defining event. Bombs dropped on the city's historic center destroyed whole blocks. Stories are handed down about vengeful and retreating Germans massacring hundreds of civilians from Arezzo and nearby towns. Families lost loved ones in fierce battles as the Allies pushed the Nazis north toward Germany and eventual surrender. Some Aretines fought as partisans battling Hitler's armies, but others fought on the opposite side against the Allies in North Africa, Albania, Greece, the former Yugoslavia, and on the Eastern front in Russia. Another group continued to collaborate with the retreating Nazis and remained loyal to the Italian Fascist dictator Benito Mussolini (Il Duce) until the bitter end.

For many older Italians, especially those who grew up in Tuscany and can remember what Arezzo was like in 1944 and 1945, the war helped define their childhoods. Now in their 70s and 80s, these Aretines have early memories of meeting a mythical American GI who may have offered up a wondrous Hershey's chocolate bar or a British solider in a tank who had just helped liberate their hometown.

Even today, many Italians have a difficult time speaking about the early 1940s. While there are some monuments to the bitter struggle between the partisans and the Italian Fascists and their Nazi allies, these shrines are often

(*facing*) *Cassettoni* (coffered ceiling) of the Arezzo post office, representing the god Mercury, Messenger of the Gods.

(*above, top*) Pictures of victims from "Sala della Memoria" in Civitella in Valdichiana.

Letters from "Sala della Memoria" in Civitella in Valdichiana.

privately funded. The markers can be surprisingly hard to find and in disrepair. For example, the commemoration of the San Polo massacre is on private property and is unimpressive and plain. The site of the concentration camp in Anghiari languished for decades until a memorial park was built in the early twenty-first century. There is a small museum in the town of Civitella in Valdichiana (about fifteen miles from Arezzo) that commemorates the tragic events of the summer of 1944, but it is tucked away and modest.

The end of the war remains difficult for many Italians because it represents a kind of national civil war between partisans (frequently

The British Commonwealth Cemetery in Indicatore, just northwest of Arezzo, honors the more than 1,200 fallen during the Allied campaign to liberate Italy from the Fascists.

Communists or Socialists on the political left) and the Fascists (from the political right). Even seven decades later, the effects are still palpable in daily political life. Liberation Day (April 25) is a national holiday that marks the fall of Mussolini and the end of the Nazi occupation. Many former partisans are considered heroes only by the political left, but the rest of the country views them more through the lens of the Cold War struggle that followed than that of the defeat of Nazi Germany.

The British Eighth Army liberated Arezzo on July 16, 1944. There are photographs of the joyous celebrations, complete with Union Jack–draped tanks on the cobblestoned streets of the historic town center. Cemeteries honoring the Allied dead are as close to Arezzo as the neighboring town of Foiano della Chiana. Much larger monuments are located at the American cemetery and memorial in Florence. The seventy-acre site holds tributes to and graves of more than forty-four hundred American soldiers who died battling the Nazis between Rome and the Alps.

The Postwar Boom

The Italy (as well as Tuscany and Arezzo) that emerged after the World War II, however, was impoverished and destroyed. The country's infrastructure had been devastated by the conflict. There were severe food shortages and a lack of

The American Cemetery in Florence is the final resting place for more than 4,400 U.S. soldiers killed in Italy during World War II. (Photo by Suzette Grillot)

adequate shelter in the first winters after the war. Many cities and towns had been severely damaged by Allied bombing and shelling from both sides. Marshall Plan loans and foodstuffs from the United States eventually helped Italy regain its economic footing. American and British troops remained on Italian soil following the German surrender. The United States still has military installations in Italy (the closest to Arezzo is in Pisa), and more than ten thousand U.S. troops are based in the country. Just as it had been for more than two thousand years, Tuscany remained largely rural and agricultural (growing grapes and olive oil) with a sprinkling of small family businesses and craftsmen.

As the country regained some semblance of normalcy in the 1950s, the Italian economy boomed. As a result of this economic miracle, the 1950s and early 1960s are literally called "the boom years" (*gli anni del boom*). The economy grew at around 6 percent annually for more than a decade. Small family-owned companies exploded in Tuscany as their products such as food, textiles, jewelry, and clothing became internationally known. Tuscan companies such as Ferragamo, Piaggio-Vespa, and Bertolli became global brand names. To this day, Italy has a larger proportion of small firms (fewer than ten employees) than any other industrialized country.

Complementing the postwar economic boom was a steady increase in tourism from abroad. While foreigners had always been intrigued by Italy, the post-1960 jet age made travel cheaper and more convenient. The advent of the Boeing 747 and intercontinental travel, coupled with new money in the United States, Japan, and across much of Western Europe, led to floods of tourists, expatriates and owners of second homes who found Tuscany a nice place to visit or live. Tuscany today accounts for 10 percent of the lucrative Italian tourism industry. Florence, alone, receives more than ten million visitors a year.

The Politics of the Red Belt in the Cold War

In the immediate aftermath of World War II, political governance in Arezzo, as in much of Italy, included the political parties that had opposed the Fascists. Tuscany would become a core part of Italy's red belt (*cintura rossa*), which made a loop around the middle of the peninsula and also included the regions of Emilia-Romagna, Umbria, and the Marches. Throughout the Cold War period, these "red" regions usually voted in the plurality for the Communists, while much of the rest of the country voted for the "white" parties, which included the Christian Democrats (DC) and its allies. The first postwar elections in Arezzo showed the results of this leftward and red tilt by rewarding the Italian Communist Party (PCI) and the Italian Socialist Party (PSI) with a majority of the votes. The Christian Democrats, more pro-American and secretly financed by the Central Intelligence Agency (CIA), also had the support of the Roman Catholic Church. The Christian Democrats had significant political support in Arezzo, but were not the dominant political force they were in many other parts of the country.

Due to Cold War pressures emanating from Washington and Moscow, Italy settled into an uneasy political pattern. The Christian Democrats won the first countrywide Italian elections in 1948 and from then on formed a series of unstable coalition governments that dominated the national political scene until the early 1990s. The Italian Communist Party became the foremost example of European communism. Under the charismatic leadership of Enrico Berlinguer in the 1970s and

1980s, the Italian Communists endorsed anti-Soviet concepts such as the North Atlantic Treaty Organization (NATO) and free-market economics, trying to find a "third way" between the West and the Soviet Union. Despite these moves toward moderation, the United States viewed European communism as a dangerous possibility that might tilt Western Europe toward the Soviets. The Italian Communists were actively shut out from holding the reins of national political power despite receiving more than a third of the national vote by the mid-1970s and coming within striking distance of the popular vote of the Christian Democrats.

At the regional and local levels, especially in the red belt that included Arezzo, Communists and Socialists were largely left alone by the great powers fighting the Cold War to govern the cities, towns, and regions. The Town Council of Arezzo chose Socialist mayors almost without interruption from 1946 through the early 1990s. Aldo Ducci, a Socialist who was mayor of Arezzo for twenty-eight of the thirty-two years between 1963 and 1995, had been jailed for his political activities during World War II. Like other red-belt cities and regions, Arezzo was known for its excellent social services, such as elementary education, sanitation, and local and regional transport systems, which still exist today.

The Years of Lead, Licio Gelli, and the Fall of the Postwar Political System

Italy's political life took a dark turn beginning in the late 1960s. The "years of lead" (*gli anni del piombo*), so called because of the terrorism, bombings, and kidnappings that claimed thousands of lives, were often random and senseless. Secretive groups on the extreme left, such as the Red Brigades (Brigate Rosse), and the extreme right, such as the neo-Fascist New Order (Ordine Nuove), claimed responsibility for heinous actions, including the kidnapping and execution of Italian Prime Minister Aldo Moro in 1978 and the Bologna train station bombing in 1980 that killed eighty-five and wounded two hundred. Terrorism paralyzed Italian society and led many to believe that the government (with an assist or at least a blind eye from the American diplomatic and intelligence communities) deliberately developed a strategy of tension (*strategia della tensione*) in order to keep the country in near chaos, thus scaring the electorate toward the safety of political moderation.

One incident in particular led Arezzo to play an important role in the politics of these years. In March 1981, Italian police raided the Arezzo villa of right-wing financier Licio Gelli. Police uncovered details about the super-secret Propaganda Due (P2) Masonic Lodge that included a list of nearly one thousand individuals, among them prominent politicians, military and intelligence officials, journalists, and businessmen. Silvio Berlusconi, then just a Milanese cable television and real-estate magnate, who would only later become a dominant figure in Italian politics and media, was listed on the P2 rolls. Propaganda Due alarmed the Italian public because it appeared to constitute a shadow right-wing state within a state. Its cloak-and-dagger activities, operations, and financing had tentacles that reached everywhere, including to a Vatican banking scandal, illegal political bribes, right-wing dictatorships in South America, and domestic terrorism, among others.

Police searching Gelli's Arezzo villa found memos outlining what Italy might look like if the P2 implemented a political-military takeover of the country. Gelli became a national villain and fled the country, eventually turning himself in to

Swiss authorities after several years on the run. Later, while serving under house arrest in Arezzo, Gelli again vanished before being sentenced to jail. He was finally apprehended on the French Riviera and extradited back to Italy.

The P2 scandal was a forerunner to a series of even larger scandals that brought down the postwar Italian political party (*partitocrazia*) system in the early 1990s. The system collapsed under a web of corruption (*tangentopoli*) as the newly emboldened Italian judiciary uncovered bribes that had permeated nearly every facet of national Italian political life. The Christian Democrats, Socialists, and many of their Allied political parties fell apart, along with much of the leadership of the country, discredited by scandal, bribery, and lies. The Communists, who had been excluded from power since the end of World War II, fared somewhat better, since they had been unable to exercise government control over the spoils system. The left, however, had to deal with its own definitional issues (including what to call themselves), given the collapse of the Soviet Union and the fall of communism. As the country tried to reform its political process in the 1990s, the regional, provincial, and municipal governments grew in strength and power, much to the benefit of cities like Arezzo.

Arezzo Today and the Fanfani Family

The Province of Arezzo (Provincia di Arezzo), which is similar to a county in the United States, comprises the easternmost section of Tuscany. It has about 350,000 inhabitants and incorporates 39 smaller towns such as Cortona, Montevarchi, Sansepolcro, and Castiglion Fiorentino. Arezzo serves as the district capital, where a president of the province presides over an elected council with administrative responsibility for issues

Palazzo della Provincia.

Sala del Consiglio (town council chamber).

The mayor's office in the Sala della Giunta (local government town hall).

Sala del Saracino (town hall conference room).

that include the environment, water and energy sources, highways, hunting and fishing, waste disposal, school buildings, and artistic heritage. At the municipal level, the city of Arezzo (Comune di Arezzo) has a mayor and an elected council who supervise public services, economic development, town planning, and local elections. The provincial president and the mayor serve five-year terms and must receive absolute majorities. Since 1995, the mayoralty of Arezzo has been alternatively held by the Berlusconi-led dominant center right party (Forza Italia) and, more recently, by the center left party (Partito Democratico) that included the former mayor, Giuseppe Fanfani.

Fanfani is one of the great political names in postwar Italian history. The Fanfanis are an important part of Arezzo's history. Amintore Fanfani, born in Pieve Santo Stefano near Arezzo in 1908, was one of the great leaders of the post–World War II era. He served six different stints as prime minister of Italy, the first two in the 1950s, two more in the 1960s, and a final two during brief periods in the 1980s. The elder Fanfani was a Christian Democrat, and, as was common during the Cold War, all but one of his six turns as prime minister lasted a year or less. Amintore Fanfani also served on the cabinets of foreign affairs, agriculture, interior, and labor, and ended his more than five decades in politics as one of the powerful senators-for-life.

The most dominant political figure in Arezzo during much of the first decade and a half of the

Pier Luigi Bersani, shown campaigning in Arezzo, was the secretary of the center-left Partido Democratico from 2009 to 2013.

The Arezzo post office.

twenty-first century was Giuseppe Fanfani, the nephew of the late prime minister. Mayor Fanfani presided over the city council, located in the middle of Arezzo on a street previously named after his famous political uncle. A lawyer by training, Mayor Fanfani first served in Rome in the lower house of the Italian Parliament as part of the center-left coalition. Elected mayor of Arezzo in 2006 and then reelected to a second five-year term in 2011, Mayor Fanfani is known to quote Dante to foreign visitors in his elegant and modernly furnished offices in the Comune building.

Fanfani stepped down as mayor in 2014 in order to take a prestigious position as a magistrate judge in Rome, leaving Vice-Mayor Stefano Gasperini at the helm. In the most recent election, which took place in May 2015, the center-right coalition party once again took over the reins of power, in direct contrast to Italy's young prime minister from the center-left party, Matteo Renzi, the former mayor of Florence.

The citizens of Arezzo care deeply about their hometown and want to make sure that it cuts a good image (*bella figura*) within Italy, both to foreign businesses and investors and to the thousands of tourists who visit the city each year. Maintaining the unique heritage of Arezzo for generations to come is more than just good governance; it makes excellent political and economic sense as well. By preserving the town's unique identity and heritage while fully integrating into the twenty-first-century world, Arezzo is well positioned to continue to thrive.

Political posters in Arezzo in support of Florence's mayor Matteo Renzi during his national campaign to lead the center-left Partito Democratico. Renzi became the prime minister of Italy in 2014 at the age of thirty-nine.

View from Collina di San Donato
(Hill of San Donato).

Part II Language, Business, and Immigration

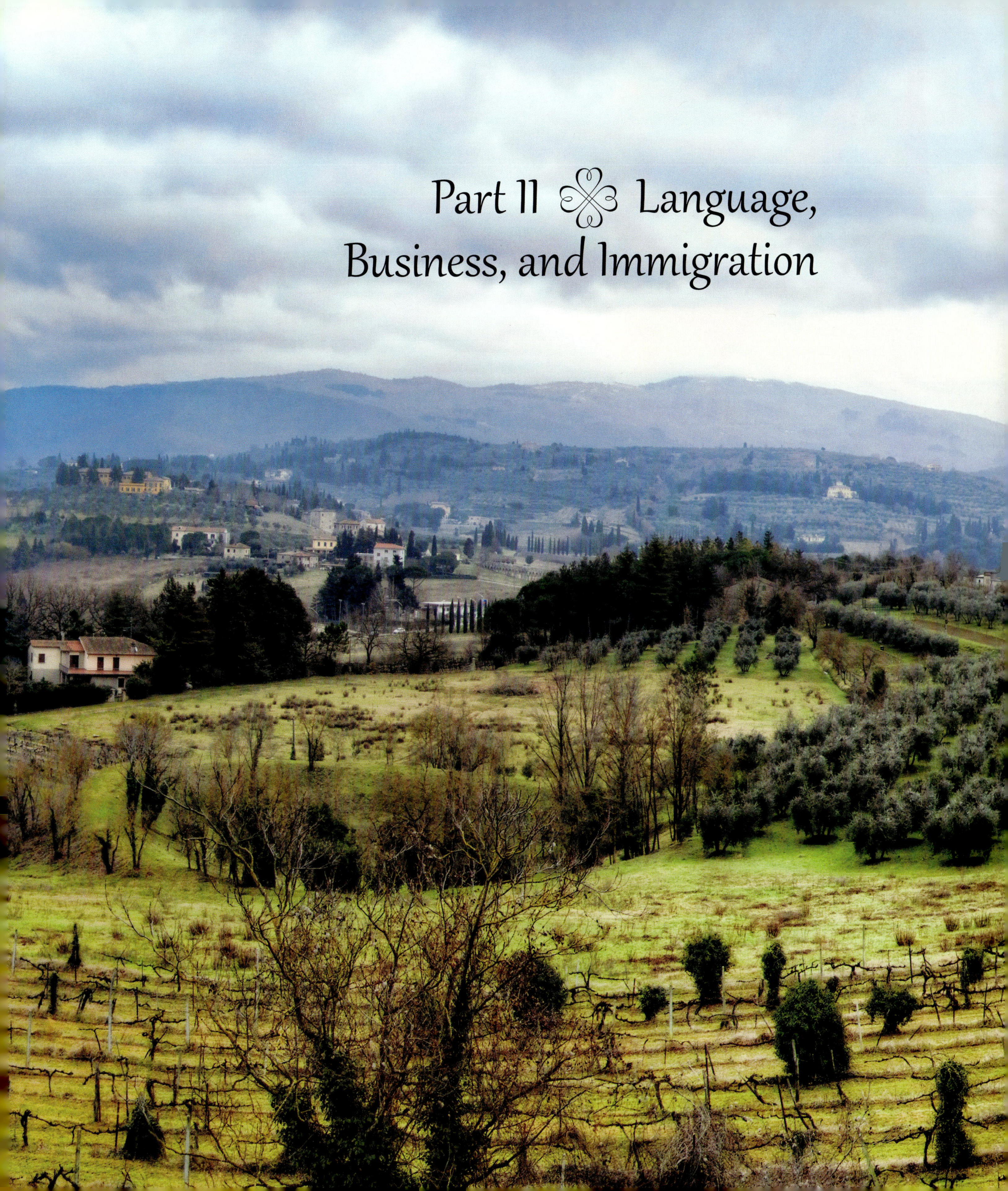

Arezzo's city walls date to the mid-sixteenth century
and defended the city from external attacks.

5

Getting to Know the Aretines

Federico Siniscalco

Through the centuries, Italy has attracted scores of foreign travelers. In the Middle Ages, they came as pilgrims to visit St. Peter's Basilica. During the seventeenth and eighteenth centuries, young aristocrats, accompanied by their tutors, traveled to Italy to complete their education by undertaking the "Grand Tour" of the sights and monuments of the classical world and the Renaissance. During the nineteenth and twentieth centuries, foreign artists and writers flocked to the Italian peninsula, attempting to follow the paths of Dante, Petrarch, Leonardo, and Michelangelo. In more recent years, enterprising tour guides have herded flocks of tourists around the country. Through all these periods, visitors have come to Arezzo, even though the stop often required a detour from the main routes connecting Florence, Siena, and Rome.

Many of these travelers from abroad created detailed records of their visits through letters, sketches, journal entries, or more elaborate travel books. Today, these records constitute a literature that offers a valuable testimonial of how foreigners viewed Italy. Most of the descriptions reflect the spirit of the age in which they were produced. Johann Wolfgang von Goethe (1794–1832), for example, was attracted to classical art works. Others, such as the British critic and intellectual John Ruskin (1819–1900), dwelled on medieval art by highlighting the so-called primitive painters. Almost all, however, concentrated on the sights, the artworks, and the landscapes, rather than the people. In fact, the local population was often seen as an obstacle to the proper appreciation of the arts and culture of Italy.

The way these tourists viewed Italy is similar to how they first saw Arezzo. Painters such as Vasari or other minor masters of the high Renaissance attracted early visitors to Arezzo. However, works by local artists, for example, the frescoes by Piero della Francesca—today one of the major reasons why tourists visit Arezzo—were hardly mentioned by travelers before the twentieth century. The local people were often described as ignorant and unrefined (Nathaniel Hawthorne lamented that no one knew about Petrarch's house in town), superstitious and bigoted (Lady Sidney Morgan described the city's inhabitants as religious fanatics for rebelling against the French Jacobins), or lazy and unkempt (Otto Speyer arrived in town and was so disturbed by the people he saw in the streets that he immediately headed for a friend's villa in the countryside).

However, the literary descriptions of Arezzo and the landscape were much more generous. Henry James wrote in *Italian Hours* of his positive feelings toward Arezzo, a town with a Medici fortress turned into a vegetable garden, and an impressive cathedral surrounded by a park from where he could admire beautiful Tuscan hills, complete with cypresses, vineyards, fruit trees, and fields of wheat. Many other writers have also praised the city—among them George Dennis, Walter Pater, Vernon Lee, Edward Hutton, André Suarès—each finding remarkable history and beauty in the city's numerous works of art. Almost every travel description of Arezzo also respectfully mentions its illustrious citizens: Gaius Maecenas, patron of the arts; Petrarch; Guido Monaco, the inventor of musical notation; and Giorgio Vasari, Renaissance artist and author of the *Lives of the Most Excellent Painters, Sculptors, and Architects.*

Even though Arezzo fared well in the descriptions written by most of its foreign visitors, they do reveal one serious limitation: those accounts were usually based on rather short visits. Most authors stopped only for a brief time and did not take the opportunity to get to really know the inhabitants of the city. Unlike other Tuscan cities such as Florence or Siena, Arezzo represented a brief respite from the real destination. Tobias Smollett, the eighteenth-century author of a famous travel book on Italy, stopped for barely two hours, just enough time for his carriage to be fixed. Today's study abroad students, or anyone else who has the possibility of a more leisurely stay, can get to know the Aretines on a much deeper level. A longer stay is the only way to get to know the *genius loci*, or the true spirit of Arezzo.

Integrating with the locals and being accepted is challenging. One of the primary characteristics of Italian towns is that, until the nineteenth century, walls surrounded them. Today, most of these walls, usually constructed during the Middle Ages, have been destroyed. However, a careful traveler will be able to see some large sections that remain standing. Arriving by train in Arezzo is not very helpful for visualizing the old city's confines, since the station stands in an area from which the original walls were almost completely removed. Any other approach, however, by car, bike, or on foot, clearly reveals the old ramparts. Most foreign writers likely approached the city by horse carriage and duly mentioned the historic walls. Today, the most striking view of the old walls is from the north, where escalators take visitors from a communal parking lot to the highest part of town, near the cathedral and the city hall.

These centuries-old walls had a great impact on Italian cities like Arezzo. To be a resident of an Italian town is to be part of an enclosed and unique community, which generates an attitude

City walls.

of suspicion and rivalry toward anyone outside that enclosed world. Belonging to a confined environment also spurred a sense of uniqueness, and the belief that the local traditions were better than those of the neighboring towns, or that local people were more industrious than those who came from somewhere else. These rivalries and suspicions go back to the hostility and warfare between the *Comuni*, the small city-states that developed in Italy during the Middle Ages. Of course, these town-centered bonds have grown weaker today as technology and transportation have shortened the distance between people and cities, but a watchful traveler can still find vestiges of the old divisions.

An outsider moving to Arezzo, even from within Italy, is perceived as someone who belongs to a different community, a different campanile. The general sense of competition that the locals once felt toward neighboring cities and towns remains palpable. It is particularly pronounced against Florence, a city that defeated Arezzo at the battle of Campaldino in 1289 (where the Florentine Dante fought). Florence subjugated Arezzo for several centuries thereafter. Grudges are still held against Siena, a wealthier and more aristocratic city. There are even jealousies against Cortona, whose tourist business bloomed earlier and remains more profitable than Arezzo's smaller niche market. Generally, though, the Aretines have a good deal of self-confidence. According to the locals, everything is better in Arezzo: from

A hand-drawn eighteenth-century family tree of the Albergotti family.

the way they make *ribollita*, the Tuscan vegetable soup, to the way they organize their joust (as compared to the Sienese *Palio*). Arezzo is a tightly knit community, and assimilation is difficult for anyone perceived as an outsider.

Another consequence of growing up within city walls is the tendency to develop exclusive, lifelong friendships. *La comitiva* translates as a group of friends who spend large amounts of time together. These special groups are formed among high school friends, but can often start as early as elementary school. Fairly large in size—up to ten or fifteen people—the numbers tend to grow even bigger as members develop their own families. There are many occasions for the group to get together: holidays, celebrations, and vacations. Among young people, daily outings are quite common. The organization of Italian schools also fosters the formation of these cliques. In each of the three major levels—elementary, middle, and high school—the students are obliged to sit within a single class, while it is the teachers who move from room to room. Year after year, the students who make up a class establish very strong ties, which often last beyond the school years.

Being an adult from a different town often makes it very difficult to be welcomed within one of these circles that began bonding in elementary school. The Aretines, like most Italians, are friendly and outgoing in casual interaction with strangers, but to be accepted in a group and become a permanent member with ties that go beyond a superficial level can be a challenge. Children can help break down some of these barriers, allowing for closer contact with other parents. In my own case, it was strangely my American wife who opened the most doors. She posed less of a threat to the local campanilismo than an Italian from another region of the country. The stereotypes that some Italians hold about Americans—culturally naïve, not knowing how to dress, spreading their overcooked pasta on sandwiches—are less menacing than those about southern Italians such as myself (who are sometimes thought of as Mafiosi, lazy, untrustworthy, unclean, and loud).

Most Italians spend their entire life in the place where they were born. The Aretines are similarly not very geographically mobile. Indeed, those who have left their hometown have more often than not chosen to do so for economic reasons. At different times in Italian history, hardship and lack of jobs have forced people to look for opportunities far from home. Today, however, most of the young people from Arezzo look for jobs as close to home as possible. Florence is an acceptable option, but only because its distance allows for a daily commute on the train. Aretines perceive travel as a temporary, leisure, or job-related experience, rather than as a permanent relocation.

Aretines and Italians are also hemmed in by the national university system. Residential universities are a rarity in Italy, and most students live at home while studying for their degree. If their hometown has no university, young Italians will often commute on a daily or weekly basis to nearby campuses. In Arezzo, there is a small branch campus of the University of Siena with limited course offerings. Most students from Arezzo travel to Florence, Siena, or Perugia on a daily basis for their studies. Some will go as far as Bologna, where they might spend the week but still come home for the weekend to enjoy home-cooked meals and the company of their childhood friends. The experience of going away to college is rare in Italy. Graduating from high school does not necessarily coincide with leaving home.

The concept of a university campus as a self-sufficient academic community is also foreign to Italian culture. For example, the students who do enroll at the University of Siena in Arezzo (about 250 per year) limit their university experience to class attendance and examinations. They spend the rest of the time either studying at home or socializing with their high school friends. The opportunity to make new friends and broaden one's social horizons while attending college is not a part of the Italian university experience. Students rely on their own cliques and families for socializing, which only reinforces an attitude of closure towards outsiders.

Young Italians tend to live at home with their parents until well into their thirties. This is true in Arezzo as well, where the *mammoni* ("mama's boy") phenomenon is alive and well. Along with the characteristics of Italian universities and the reluctance to move away from home, other reasons include the scarcity of jobs and the insufficiency of affordable housing. Family remains a defining institution in Italian culture, and in its extended form (siblings, parents, grandparents, aunts, uncles, and cousins of various degrees), it offers a sense of security to the Aretines. Large family gatherings for official holidays (Christmas, Easter) are typical. Celebrations of christenings, first communions, university graduations, and weddings are also cause for gathering and festivity. The family is sometimes more open to outsiders than the school groups. Foreigners visiting Arezzo and new immigrants who have left their own families behind are often invited to partake in family celebrations and gatherings. These are wonderful experiences and should not be missed, because they are the best way for an outsider to learn more about local customs, food, and drink.

The University of Siena branch campus in Arezzo.

Arezzo's families help out with daily life in ways that might seem foreign to the outsider. Because schools are usually open only in the mornings, working parents often leave their children in the custody of the grandparents. Families also play an essential role in helping others when someone gets sick. It is not uncommon for family members to care for their loved ones in hospitals and clinics, which are often understaffed with nursing and personal caregivers. Family life can also be stressful. Homes are small and siblings often share bedrooms, ensuring that most family life takes place within a confined environment. Many of the local youngsters end up spending quite a bit of time in the city's open spaces: parks, piazzas, and most of all, Corso Italia, historically Arezzo's most important street. The Corso is where one of the city's most intriguing

(*facing*) Corso Italia.

Friends gather at Tuscanative, a local food, wine, and bike shop, to enjoy a drink, antipasti, and good company.

occurrences takes place: the habitual afternoon stroll, or *passeggiata*.

The custom of taking a leisurely afternoon walk in one of the local streets or piazzas is an old tradition that continues in most Italian cities and towns. Many foreign travelers who described Italy in their journals and books were taken by the phenomenon of the afternoon stroll. Nathaniel Hawthorne and his wife, Sophia, both wrote in detail of how elegant and attractive the people of Arezzo seemed as they promenaded on the sunny and well-tended Corso. Even today foreign visitors are puzzled by the large numbers of people who gather in the afternoons to carry out their *vasche* (the term, used locally, and best translated as "pool laps" to describe the tracing and retracing of a particular stretch of a local street). People gather along the Corso around four in the afternoon and remain on the street until just before dinnertime. Though dominated by the young people who walk within their groups, there are some older and well-tailored citizens as well. Girls walk with other girls, and boys walk with boys. While many nervous glances may be exchanged, not much else takes place. The interaction is somewhat limited, especially among strangers. This is the norm in Italy, where only after a formal introduction will people acknowledge each other in the streets. Mostly people are there to make a "good impression" or "*fare bella figura*." Once upon a time, a passeggiata required formal dress with only the best clothes. Today, the regular stroll is more about showing an affinity to a cultural subgroup and to see one's neighbors. In truth, some of the local youth are quite critical of the vasche and try to pursue alternative pastimes in the afternoon, such as practicing sports or getting involved in music, theater, or other extracurricular activities.

For a foreigner planning to spend a significant period in town, or for an Italian moving in from a different city, the afternoon walk is not the best way to meet the locals. It is entertaining, however, to watch the Aretines go through their paces. An easier approach may be to seek out Aretines at restaurants, bars, and cafés. The Aretines, like most Italians, are well versed in the art of casual conversation. With a bit of persistence, and some time at one's disposal, it is possible to break through the initial reservation. While it may take a serious effort, it will open the path to understanding to those fortunate enough to reside in this magical city.

Guido Antolini, visiting from Rome, enjoys dinner with a colleague at one of the many Arezzo restaurants.

CVM OXORE
ANOS XX

6

Italian Language Today

Jason Houston

In Arezzo they speak Italian . . . and Hindi, and Arabic, and Romanian, and German, and, even if Italian-language students deny it, they speak some English as well. Arezzo fully participates in the globalizing Babelic mixture of languages that resounds in cities around the world. A trip up Corso Italia during the evening passeggiata is complete with elegant Tuscans of a certain age carrying on in the muddy Aretine dialect as well as sophisticated young men and women speaking educated Italian, all while a patois of English and Italian, which often makes no sense in either language, seeps from the storefronts.

Arezzo, however, is a true Italian city, situated near Florence, the city that birthed the dialect that has become standard Italian. Professors teach Florentine Italian in classrooms from Palermo to Turin, as well as from Sydney, Australia, to Anchorage, Alaska. Thus, Aretines pride themselves on their place near the center of the Italian language universe, celebrating the historical importance of their most famous son, Francesco Petrarch, one of the fathers of Italian language and literature. At the same time, Aretines hold something of a grudge against their more famous neighbors in Florence. Arezzo's dialect varies from the purity of the Florentine more than other Tuscan cities like Siena and Pisa; but the difference also generates civic pride. This paradox, known as *La Questione della Lingua* (The Language Question), resides at the heart of Italian language and society. The debate has evolved over the past eight hundred years from a question of Latin versus the vernacular (Italian dialects) to arbitrary value judgments placed on the merit of particular Italian dialects. More

(*facing*) An Aretine artifact exhibited in the Archaeological Museum of Arezzo.

recently, scholars, writers, and others have embraced the differences in regional dialects, insisting on their place in the curriculum in public schools. There is a great deal of ground to cover, so, as the Aretines might say, "*Alò citti!*" ("Hey, guys, let's get going!")

Italian is a Romance language, which means it developed from Latin. This does not mean that learning to speak Italian should be easy for the student of Classical Latin. Indeed, while Latin is the root of Italian, many elements have had an impact on Italian. This variety, combined with the natural way languages change over time, has created today's idiom. Foreign invasions have introduced words unknown in Latin. The Lombards in the sixth century gave Italian words such as *banca* (bank), *palco* (stage), and *scherzare* (to joke). The rise of American culture and mass media, as well as digital communications, in the late twentieth century added words such as *cliccare* (to click on a link), *sport*, and *twittare* (to tweet). Modern Italian has absorbed words from neighbors and from languages around the planet, but it remains fundamentally an Italic artifact, resonant of the history of the boot-shaped peninsula and of the idea of the nation of Italy.

During the Classical Roman period over two thousand years ago and also in the modern nation-state of Italy, founded less than two hundred years ago, the peoples inhabiting the peninsula have spoken many forms of Italian. Some are separate languages altogether; for example, Friulian (northeast Italy) and Sicilian (extreme southern Italy). Many of these regional varieties are dialects, closely related to standard Italian but with their own unique aspects of grammar and vocabulary. The Neapolitan dialect is a specific version throughout southern Italy. Within regions and specific language groups, different places have distinct accents, local vocabulary, and pronunciations that distinguish people from different parts, such as in Tuscany. Marta Agnelli of Arezzo tells of her confusion when her grandfather used a local exclamation, *ìe*, to mean "yes," when that same word can mean "not at all" in Arezzo. Astonishingly, her grandfather lives fifteen miles away from Arezzo, in the town of Castiglion Fiorentino. As Agnelli explains, the meaning of this word changes depending on context, gesture, and place.

Written records show that such variation has existed since the creation of the Italian language. The earliest written instances of a language distinct from Latin appeared in the late tenth century. The earliest examples of Italian dialects are not literary texts, but rather legal documents such as property deeds, wills, and contracts. Other examples appear in more literary contexts: a riddle written in the margins of a manuscript by a bored monk, or doodled translations of Latin phrases. They help illustrate the seemingly independent development of many Italian dialects across the peninsula.

One unique example explains why the vernacular struggled to gain traction in writing during the Middle Ages. A twelfth-century fresco in the Basilica of Saint Clement in Rome contains inscriptions in Italian that hold the key to a greater understanding of the birth of the modern Italian language. The frescoes tell the story of Saint Sissinius, who, speaking in Latin, ordered around some pagan workmen. These fellows, crude and uneducated, did not speak proper Latin, but rather grunted in the "vulgar." "*Falite dereto colo palo Carvoncelle . . . Gosmari, Albertel, traite. File de le pute, traite.*" ("Push him from behind with your stick Carvoncello . . . Gosmari, Albertel, pull. You sons of bitches, pull!") Beyond the blushingly filthy language contained in this fresco of the saint's life—located in a church, no

Detail from the Stories of Saint Clement, fresco, lower church of the Basilica of Saint Clement, Rome, twelfth century. (Photo by DeAgostini / Getty Images)

less—the message for the historian of language could not be more clear: good, holy, smart people speak in Latin, while the miserable wretches of the vulgar masses speak the debased language: Italian.

In contrast, the first complete literary text in an Italian dialect comes from Italy's patron saint, Saint Francis of Assisi (1181–1226). Among his many writings that survive in his Umbrian dialect is the verse prayer "Laudes Creaturarum" (Praise for Creation), a celebration of all nature as evidence of God's love for his creation.

Laudato sie, mi' Signore, cum tucte le tue creature, spetialmente messor lo frate sole, lo qual'è iorno, et allumini noi per lui. Et ellu è bellu e radiante cum grande splendore, de te, Altissimo, porta significatione.

(Praise be my Lord, through all of your creatures, especially through Lord Brother Sun, and you illuminate us through him. And he is beautiful and radiant in his great splendor, of You, oh Highest, he brings understanding.)

This poem officially marks the beginning of Italian literature and of the particularly Italian artistic notion of nature as symbolic of the divine. However, the poem, written in a language without standardized grammar or spelling, still shows traces of Latin (*cum* instead of *con*, *tucte* instead of *tutte*) and seemingly random discrepancies that a modern grammar teacher would abhor (such as using *bello* and *bellu* interchangeably).

With so much variation in language and dialect, how can there be a standard Italian language? Amazingly, there is a clear and easy answer to this question: Dante Alighieri. Dante (1265–1321) was a Florentine poet, politician, and philosopher (among other pursuits) who championed the cause of establishing one version of the many Italian vernacular (non-Latin) dialects. In his treatise *De Vulgari Eloquentia* (On the Eloquence of the Vernacular), Dante rewrites the history of language by discarding the biblical Babelic language theory, which holds that all language variation arises from the prideful sin of King Nimrod, and instead arguing that linguistic variation is a natural result of languages developing as humans speak them over time. He then goes through many of the

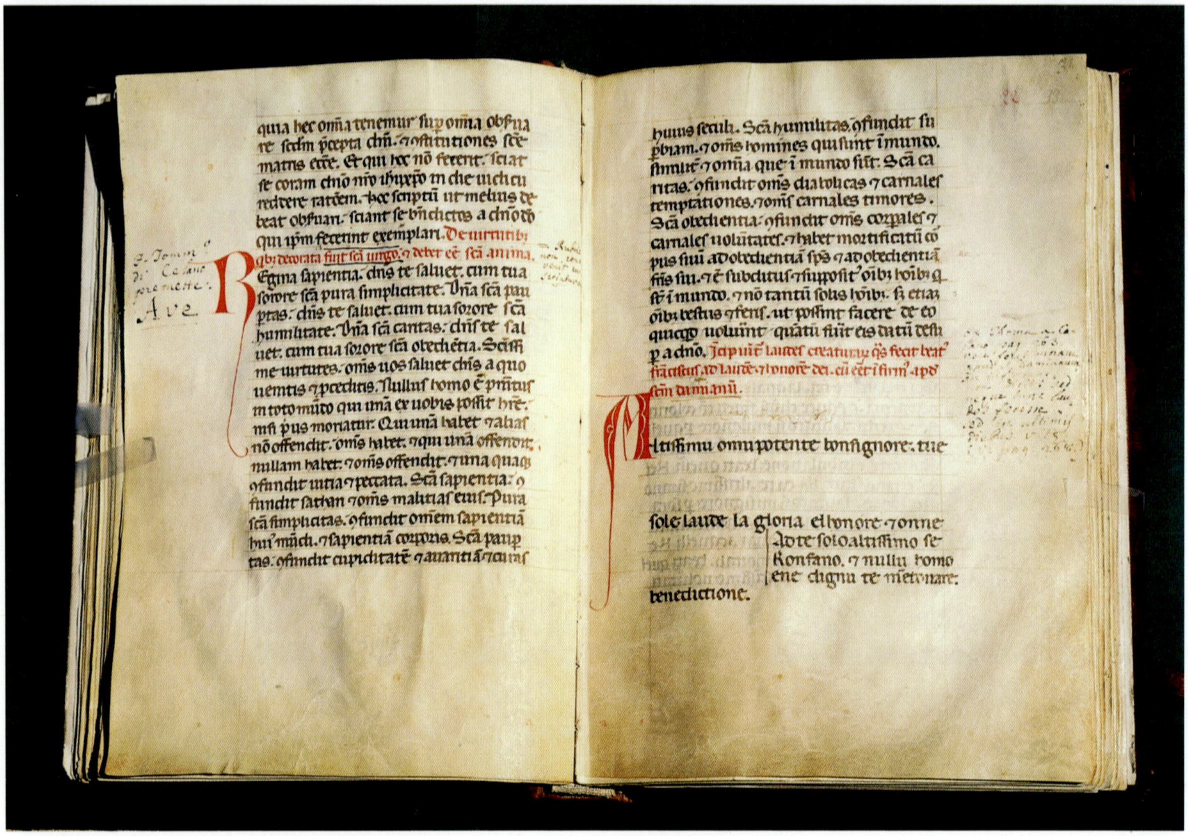

Canticle of the Sun, or the Canticle of Brother Sun, by Francis of Assisi (1181–1226), pages from a fourteenth-century manuscript. Assisi, Biblioteca Comunale. (Photo by DeAgostini / Getty Images)

existing dialects to find one which is properly illustrious (*illustre*), prominent (*cardinale*), noble (*aulico*), and courtly (*curiale*) to use in poetry and elegant speech. After dismissing many Italian dialects for their various defects (for example, the Roman dialect is a "vile jargon" as ugly as the Romans themselves; those from Aquilea "belch forth" their language; etc.), Dante settles on the Tuscan dialect as spoken in Florence, his mother tongue. Dante's motive for promoting a single unified Italian language is both linguistic and political; nobody speaks Latin as a mother tongue, so writing in Latin is forced and artificial. Because politically diverse languages lead to political fragmentation and weakness, there is a need for a shared linguistic bond.

Dante's little treatise on Italian, written in Latin so that the educated elites of his day would pay attention, reveals the theoretical underpinnings that motivated his choice to write his poetic masterpiece, *The Divine Comedy*, in Italian. The influence of his epic poem made his theory a reality. While there had been earlier poets writing in the Florentine dialect, the breathtaking artistic accomplishment of *La Commedia* made Dante's Italian the preeminent language of the Italian peninsula. In *La Commedia*, Dante combined erudite poetic, philosophical, scientific, and theological knowledge with beautiful, idiomatic, and clear poetry in the Florentine vernacular. Perhaps the scope of his accomplishment is best illustrated by the fact that his poem was translated, at least in part, into Latin by papal prelates only decades after his death.

DANTE

DE LA VOLGARE

ELOQUENZIA.

Giovanni di Boccaccio da Certaldo, ne la vita di Dante.

Appresso gia vicino a la sua Morte compose un Libretto in prosa latina, il quale elli intitulò. De vulgari Eloquentia; E come che per lo detto libretto apparisca lui havere in animo di distinguerlo, e di terminarlo in quattro libri, o che piu non ne facesse da la Morte soprapreso, o che perduti siano gli altri, piu non ne appariscono, che i dui primi.

De Vulgari Eloquentia (On the Eloquence of the Vernacular), treatise by Dante Alighieri (1265–1321), title page of a 1529 edition. Padova, Biblioteca Civica. (Photo by DeAgostini / Getty Images)

The success of Dante's *La Commedia* spurred imitation, and his choice to compose in the Tuscan vernacular set the new standard for literary composition in cities and courts around Italy. While the clerics and other educated elites continued to refine their Latin, Tuscan was the language of the broader Italian culture. Two Tuscan followers of Dante, Giovanni Boccaccio (1313–75, born in Certaldo between Florence and Siena) and Francesco Petrarch (1304–73, born in Arezzo), took up Dante's challenge to compose refined, classically inspired literary texts in the Tuscan dialect. Boccaccio, in particular, played an active role in the diffusion and advancement of Tuscan as the literary language of all of Italy by writing his prose masterpiece, *The Decameron*, in Tuscan. Boccaccio's collection of a hundred stories created a more concrete literary language. He spent years refining his book, attempting to reduce variation in word forms and grammar. Moreover, through his efforts as a *Dantista* (a scholar and promoter of Dante), he argued far and wide for the preeminence of the Tuscan language of Dante, and, of course, of his own *Decameron*.

Arezzo's own literary giant, Francesco Petrarch, had a more ambiguous relationship with his native language. While most readers, both during Petrarch's day and during our own, know the exquisitely polished Italian poems that make up his *Canzoniere*, Petrarch himself considered these poems trifle compared to his Latin literary productions. Even more problematic, although he understood his poetry to be indebted to Dante's, in a letter to Boccaccio he professed something close to disdain for Dante's choice to write for the "vulgar herd" in Italian. Yet, despite his protestations, Petrarch's poems are careful, elegant, and precise jewels that expand the expressive meaning of the nascent Italian language through a purification of linguistic form. Petrarch's poetry elevates and formalizes the Tuscan language, allowing later authors to refer to his poems almost as a thesaurus of poetic images. Like Boccaccio's prose, Petrarch's poetry built upon Dante's linguistic and artistic foundation in *La Commedia* to extend the range of the language while codifying its usage.

Petrarch and Boccaccio represent an important development from Dante's founding effort to establish Tuscan as standard Italian, and they were certainly cognizant of their relationship to Dante, as well as their influence on their own generation of writers and those that would follow. However, it was Cardinal Pietro Bembo (1470–1547) who would formally solidify the positions of these three Florentine literary crowns (*tre corone fiorentine*). Bembo was from Venice, but his literary, cultural, and political interests led him to the same conclusion that Dante had formulated two centuries earlier: Tuscan should become the standard Italian. Bembo wrote his treatise, *Prosa della vulgar lingua* (Essay on the Vernacular), to canonize Dante, Petrarch, and Boccaccio as the fathers of the Italian language and as models for all writing.

Bembo likely had a specific type of reader in mind when he composed this essay. His fellow politician and intellectual, Baldassare Castiglione (1478–1529), had recently argued in his own literary work, *Il Cortegiano* (The Courtier), that the dominance of the Tuscan vernacular in Italian culture was an unnecessary and harmful affectation. He craftily borrowed Dante's own rationale for the Tuscan language to argue that writing in the language of Petrarch or Boccaccio would be unnatural for a Mantuan like himself living two hundred years later. He complained that even contemporary Tuscans sound artificial attempting to speak in the antiquated literary forms of their now ancient ancestors. Castiglione's anti-Florentine linguistic stance masks a political critique of the Medici family (rulers of Florence), whom he opposed while working as an ambassador for foreign lords. Likewise, another famous son of Arezzo, Pietro Aretino, had mocked the traditionalism of the elegant Tuscan championed by Bembo by composing pornographic sonnets in the poetic language of Dante and Petrarch. The resistance to the canonization of the Tuscan dialect offered by Castiglione and Aretino represents an important shift in the language question.

From Dante to Bembo and onward to the unification of Italy in the 1860s, the language question played a major role in the ideological formulation of Italian identity. Authors such as Vittorio Alfieri from Turin, Giacomo Leopardi from the Papal States on Italy's eastern coast, Ugo Foscolo from Venice, and Alessandro Manzoni from Milan all consciously opted to Tuscanize their writing so that they could contribute to the formation of an Italian national identity through the standardization of a national language. After the unification of Italy, one of the prime roles of the national education system was to teach Italians the language that had now come to be regarded as Italian, meaning the specific Florentine dialect that Dante had chosen over six hundred years earlier. Military service, centralized government, train travel and a highway system, radio, television, and now the Internet and smart phones have all helped to create a national language, which, while certainly based on the dialect of fourteenth-century Florence, is truly national.

In Arezzo, of course, they speak Italian . . . but Aretines will tell you that their Italian is not pretty and that the purest Italian is spoken between Siena and Florence. Take that with a grain of salt. The Italian they speak in Arezzo directly descends from the Italian of Dante, Petrarch, and Boccaccio, but it is also the Italian of a modern, globalized nation-state. In Arezzo, Petrarch's house museum atop the Corso marks the spot of one of the stories from Boccaccio's *Decameron*, and Via Dante Alighieri paves the way for modern-day travelers. Every Italian city celebrates these three Tuscan authors, not just because they were poets, but also because, through their poetry, they created a language, a culture, and a nation.

Unoaerre Gold Museum.

7 Arezzo's Business Landscape

Gina London

Gold, Fashion, and Real Estate

After a long dependence on agriculture, Arezzo emerged from World War II as a developing marketplace, ready for economic growth in three major areas: gold, clothing, and, as a result of the wealth of the first two, real estate.

Unoaerre was the most important gold producer in the province. Founded in the 1920s by Leopoldo Gori and Carlo Zucchi, it was also the first goldsmith company in the province, and, as a result, was required to engrave the identification mark "1 AR" into each of its products, which evolved into the company's name. But it wasn't until after World War II, during the 1950s and 1960s, that the company reached its apex, with a global reach and as many as twelve hundred employees working in its Arezzo facilities alone. Some reports claimed that Unoaerre was, at one time, the biggest goldsmith in the world. Scores of successful gold, silver, and accessory companies followed. The Graziella Group, for example, is another Arezzo-based luxury jewelry company, started in 1958 by Graziella Buoncompagni. The high-profile company now sells its products worldwide. Arezzo's gold industry peaked in the 1980s with the launch of Oro-Arezzo, or GoldArezzo, an international trade show that is still held annually, solidifying Arezzo's position and reputation in the global market.

Along with Arezzo's postwar gold rush came the arrival of fashion. In the 1950s, Caterina Lebole, along with her two sons, transformed her small textile and fabric workshop into a fashion design and tailoring business in the center of Arezzo. By 1959, the Lebole brand was officially registered and boasted nearly fifteen hundred full-time local employees. Interestingly, many of the workers in the large facilities of Lebole and Unoaerre during this time were women. Times were changing after the war, and many Italian women became more independent and sought jobs outside of the home. Lebole took advantage of this trend, transforming dozens of independent seamstresses into its unified workforce. Unoaerre, too, capitalized on the increased presence of women in the workforce.

Just outside of Arezzo lies the little town of Sansepolcro where Fabio Inghirami founded a clothing manufacturing business in 1949. Specializing in men's shirt production, the company quickly became influential and expanded into other categories of menswear and women's clothing. The Inghirami Group now comprises a collection of companies with offices in Budapest, Shanghai, Barcelona, Paris, Dubai, and New York. Critics contend that the Inghirami Group is an example of how the prestigious "Made in Italy" label can be misleading. They claim that not all of its products bearing this seal of international approval are entirely assembled in Italy. However, Article 24 of the European Customs Code (Reg EEC 2913/1992) states that a product made in two or more countries is still considered to originate in the country where the final transformation occurred or a substantial amount of work took place, allowing Inghirami and other companies to sew a "Made in Italy" tag inside a product that may not have been completely made inside the country.

While "Made in Italy" on clothing does not necessarily mean what it is supposed to mean, pasta production is true Italian. The Fabianelli family capitalized on the Italian tradition when they started making pasta back in 1860 in the village of Castiglion Fiorentino, just a short train ride from Arezzo. The Fabianelli Group, still headed by a member of the family, is now the largest pasta maker in Arezzo, reinforced by two additional brands, Pasta Toscana and Maltagliati. The company exports 60 percent of its pasta products to grocery stores and homes all over the world, including the United States. The more famous international pasta brand, Buitoni, was also founded in the province of Arezzo, by the Buitoni family in Sansepolcro in 1827. Nestlé bought the company from the family in the 1980s and now exports its pasta to more than fifty countries.

An Economy Stuck in Neutral

The Organization for Economic Co-operation and Development (OECD) reported that Italy's economic growth rate has remained below the European average over the past decade. Italy's labor productivity is also falling compared to other large European economies, and direct foreign investment in Italy remains lower than in other countries of similar size. The World Bank places Italy sixty-fifth out of 189 countries, based on a wide range of economic criteria, including the ability and ease of conducting business. Italy's reputation for unnecessary bureaucracy, lax contract enforcement and tax collection, and limited credit often scares away foreign investors, which is not very encouraging for a country that was a founding member of the European Union. Arezzo faces similar economic challenges. The entire Tuscan region has been mired in recession for much of the past decade, with layoffs at large companies and slow declines in tourism as the international economic crisis put the brakes on leisure travel.

Unoaerre Gold Museum.

Monnalisa is a world leader in clothes and accessories for children.

While the worldwide popularity of pasta continues to climb, both Arezzo's fashion and gold industries have dropped off since the 1990s because they failed to adapt to the changing global marketplace. The spread of Italian-developed manufacturing technology and expertise in its use internationally led to the relocation of gold jewelry production to less expensive centers, such as Turkey. Unoaerre still produces gold jewelery, but fewer than five hundred employees work at its headquarters in Arezzo. However, visitors to Arezzo can tour a museum dedicated to the history of gold.

The Arezzo fashion house of Lebole endured similar hardships. Cheaper manufacturing in other countries undermined their power and income base. The Lebole family still controls the brand name, and recently earned national design headlines with its bold new jewelry. But Lebole's headquarters are now in the nearby small town of Castiglion Fibocchi, rather than in downtown Arezzo.

Some Signs of an Economic Renewal

Arezzo's Graziella Group responded to economic difficulties with more innovation and agility than other Arezzo-based companies. Still involved in jewelry, it recently opened a new holding company to produce electricity from renewable sources. Graziella Green Power is one of Italy's largest producers of solar electrical power with more than thirty sites in operation. It is also involved in the development of geothermal, bio-, and wind-powered energy.

Advancements in the service sector drive Arezzo's economy today. Chimet, based just outside of Arezzo near the tiny hillside village of Civitella in Valdichiana, is the largest company in Europe for recycling chemical waste. Founded in 1976, the company began by disposing industrial waste from the production of gold and other precious metals. Another cutting-edge company based in Arezzo is CEIA, one of the world's leading makers of security devices and metal detectors. The company's high-tech security products are used worldwide in airports, police departments, courts, and schools. In addition, the company produces heating and cleaning systems that are used globally by food, textile, and pharmaceutical industries.

Some relative newcomers to Arezzo's fashion and jewelry market landscape are also incorporating a more service-oriented and socially aware approach. Piero Iacomoni founded Monnalisa in 1968, and the Arezzo-based upscale children's clothing company now has thirty-five stores in fifty countries. The company also administers the Monnalisa Onlus Foundation, which provides humanitarian services to area schools, children, and families.

Similarly, the Arezzo architect-turned-jewelry-maker Giovanni Raspini has taken his small business global. His flagship store proudly stands on Corso Italia, where he can often be found hanging out and chatting with friends, but his work is exported internationally. Raspini sponsors local art and cultural events like Icastica, Arezzo's first annual international art competition, launched in 2013. Raspini designed and produced the festival's award statuettes. Icastica displays a variety of contemporary art from around the world throughout the city center, considered a bold move since many of the provocative works were displayed inside churches and museums alongside more traditional Renaissance art. Local reaction to the contemporary art was mixed, but the city-hosted event, which was largely financially supported by Arezzo-based bank Banca Etruria, was held in an effort to put Arezzo on the tourism

Monnalisa is a world leader in clothes and accessories for children.

Monnalisa's designers work to create this season's fashions.

map—another important potential source of income for the city.

According to the local chamber of commerce, tourists are coming in greater numbers to Arezzo, yet the city still is not as popular as Siena, its better-known Tuscan neighbor. Siena's biannual Palio medieval-themed horse-race packs in tourists from all over the world. Arezzo, which holds an equally splendid medieval-themed jousting competition twice a year, receives a fraction of the international fame and tourists. "Arezzo has as much or more to offer compared with Siena," said one local journalist, "but we haven't yet told everyone. We are less polished, but that also provides a more authentic experience." Authentic or not, international supermarkets and department stores, including giants Ipercoop and Esselunga, have given Arezzo the feel of a thriving Italian city.

No Longer Built on Gold

Gold built the framework for Arezzo's modern economy, but it has since grown more diversified and complex. Like the rest of Italy, a large proportion of Arezzo's businesses are still small and family owned. But the city hopes that diversification and global competition will push Arezzo toward a more solid economic future. Cultural events that spur tourism, innovation in the technology and services sectors, and investment in the community all point Arezzo in a positive economic direction. The future, unlike the past, will likely not be built on gold, but perhaps it will be even brighter.

Abu, from Bangladesh, sells roses at local restaurants.

8

Immigration in Arezzo

Monica Sharp

Italians have a long history of emigrating, resettling, and adapting to new countries. Hyphenated Italian communities have thrived in the United States, Canada, Argentina, and dozens of other nations for more than a century, influencing what the world thinks of Italy. Today, however, it is immigration to Italy from the developing world that is shaping how Italians view themselves.

Dramatic events in modern history set the stage for mass Italian emigration beginning in the mid-nineteenth century. Italy became a unified country in 1861 without a national popular uprising. Tuscan farmers scarcely blinked at the seismic political events taking place in distant cities like Turin. They went on with their lives, farming and harvesting, picking olives or grapes, speaking in dialect, and observing provincial customs. The unification of Italy was a political footnote for much of agricultural Italy. It is said that when Giuseppe Garibaldi, the founder of the modern Italian state, arrived in Sicily with his troops, shouting "Viva Italia!," the locals thought he was saying, "Talia," and that perhaps this was his wife's name. The story illuminates just how unfamiliar the rural citizens of the new country were to the idea of the Italian nation state.

Leaving for Greener Pastures

The political changes of the nineteenth century coincided with the Industrial Revolution and the mass migration from rural into urban areas of people seeking work. Western Europe's rapidly industrializing economies, including the new Italian nation, needed workers to power growing factories and to build the sort of infrastructure required to support an expanding economy. Transportation improvements, especially railroads and steamships, made previously arduous journeys comparatively fast and safe. European immigrants in search of work and better lives suddenly had the option of traveling to faraway cities around the world. Word of mouth traveled fast, and stories trickled back to rural Italian communities of riches to be had across the ocean.

As opportunities arrived, many Italians considered emigration, but it was not an easy decision, caught between the opportunity of a better life and the difficulty of leaving behind everything they had ever known. Many rural Italians were still truly peasants, working their own plot for subsistence or sharecropping. For a large number, the lure of opportunity won out, leading Italy to become an exit country, with as many as twenty-five million Italians choosing to leave in the second half of the nineteenth century. Four million Italians immigrated to the United States and Canada alone between 1870 and 1914. Italian immigrants also relocated to other parts of the world, forming significant communities in France, Switzerland, Germany, Brazil, Argentina, and Australia. Seasonal labor performed by Italians under the supervision of Italian *padroni* (labor bosses) was common throughout the Americas. Wages were frequently paid back to the padroni in exchange for travel costs. When the seasonal labor ended, the Italians usually returned home. For the most part, seasonal workers in faraway lands came from the southern part of Italy. Emigrating northern Italians more often went across the Alps to work seasonally in northern Europe.

Those who chose to settle permanently abroad often sent a male member of the family to establish a home in the new country before sending for the rest of the family. Seasonal and permanent immigrants formed communities of their compatriots abroad, or "Little Italys," throughout northern Europe, North America, and South America. These communities became microcosms of the specific regions in Italy from where the immigrants originally hailed. The existence of Italian communities in a host country was often the tipping point in the argument for emigration. Residents lived in communities with neighbors and family members from their respective provinces, receiving and sharing news from home. This network channeled updates regarding employment opportunities, as well as suggestions for potential marriage matches. These communities offered a close and valuable connection to hometowns and regions back in Italy.

Italian history is full of invasions and conquests, and the land was repeatedly divided through the centuries by stronger European powers, especially Spain. At the same time, frequent warfare between Italians led them to form alliances with foreigners. The northern and southern parts of the peninsula viewed each other warily across a cultural gap. Yet Italians still don't agree on where the dividing line is between the north and the south. Rome is a commonly cited demarcating line between north and south, but for a Milanese, the line may begin in the Apennine Mountains just south of Bologna. Many Romans, however, draw the line south of Naples, not far from Pompeii. This division between the purportedly "industrious" northern part of the country and the historically "more economically and politically troubled" south, or *mezzogiorno*, is an important aspect of national culture. Italians sometimes view other Italians as "foreign" if they come from different regions; for example, a native of Bolzano in the Alto Adige along the

Italian pizza is lighter than American pizza with less tomato sauce and a thin, crispy crust.

Austrian border has far more in common with German-speaking Austrians than with a native of Palermo in Sicily.

In part due to cultural assimilation and the passage of time, Italian culture abroad has eroded, leaving truncated Little Italys that are little more than tourist traps in cities as diverse as Buenos Aires, São Paulo, New York, San Francisco, and Toronto. Interestingly, these communities that are thought to represent all of Italy were often only expressions of a particular town or region of the country. For example, in New York's Little Italy, residents revere San Gennaro, the patron saint of Naples. There is a statue of San Gennaro in the neighborhood, and, since 1926, the residents have held a quintessentially Neapolitan festival celebrating the saint, which was immortalized in the film *The Godfather* during Don Corleone's famous killing of a local Mafia don.

Italian immigrants also built communities in small-town America. In Krebs, Oklahoma, for example, Italian culture has continued with third- and fourth-generation Americans. Italians began migrating to the southeast corner of the Sooner state in the early twentieth century to support the growing mining industry. As petroleum replaced coal and the mines closed, many Italian families quickly left Oklahoma, but vestiges of the once-thriving "Little Italy" still remain today in the dusty town, located about two hours southeast of Oklahoma City. St. Joseph's Catholic Church hosts an annual celebration of Our Lady of Mount Carmel, featuring a pasta dinner, Italian games, and fireworks. Annual festivals still include games of *bocce* ball (a combination of shuffleboard and bowling) and *morra* (a counting game where the goal is to call out the correct number of fingers displayed in a group of players). To this day, Krebs is well known throughout the state as a place to eat authentic Italian food and to celebrate Italian culture.

Most Little Italys around the world have a distinctly southern flavor, since many of the immigrants hailed from places like Naples, Calabria, and Sicily. The spaghetti and meatballs, the red-checked tablecloths, the pizza—all familiar to Americans as distinctly "Italian"—are, in fact, examples of southern culture. Calabrese meatballs were created to make the best of poor cuts of meat. The checkered tablecloths show a humbler side of Mediterranean dining. Pizza was invented in Naples, but is now known virtually everywhere in the world and is closely identified with Italy. Mozzarella, basil, and tomato sauce are a mouth-watering call to the colors of the Italian flag, even though it was originally a regional dish.

Italy's Failed Imperial Adventure

The Fascist dictator Mussolini, who dominated Italian political life after Word War I until his death in 1945, was obsessed with the idea of "pure" Italian "blood" and "culture." New nationalistic laws prohibited Italians from speaking local dialects, and the heavily militarized regime insisted that Italian culture change from a "soft, sympathetic" culture to a stronger, more "masculine" society that could compete with other, more-industrialized, European countries. Just as Germany tried to reach back into a mythic Aryan past, Italy likewise invoked the glorious history of the Roman Empire to support Fascist ideology. Italy's sense of betrayal at being denied the spoils of World War I promised in the Treaty of Versailles provided the impetus for Mussolini to form Italian colonies abroad, eventually creating l'Africa Orientale Italiana (Italian East Africa) in Ethiopia, Somalia, and Eritrea. Mussolini then added Libya, the purported *quarta sponda* (fourth shore) of Italy, to the new Fascist Italian Empire, along with Albania, on the other side of the Adriatic Sea.

Although Italy was a latecomer to European colonialism, *l'Impero italiano* was an important rallying cry for Fascism. The Italian government sponsored emigration to the African colonies, touting the value of resettlement of southern Italians. Many northern Italians became colonial administrators abroad. By the late 1930s, thousands of Italian immigrants lived in the African colonies, intertwining the cultures in lasting ways, despite the fact that the Allies would soon sweep Italian armies out of Africa.

After World War II, the former Italian colonies in Africa became independent, but many continued to use Italian as a second language and celebrate Italian customs and cuisine. The colonial history of Italy in Africa, combined with Italy's postwar devastation, laid the ground for many of Italy's immigration and emigration issues today. Italy does not preference Africans from former Italian colonies the same way Britain has given preference to individuals from its former colonies and spheres of influence, but the migratory channels between Italy and Africa that were formed during the colonial years persist to this day.

Arezzo and Italy as an Immigration Destination

Italy emerged from World War II a broken country, but American funding through the Marshall Plan eventually helped initiate a period of economic renewal, particularly in the industrial north. This economic boom did not extend into the south, due to the fact that the industrialization of the northern part of the country was already well established. In the three decades following the fall of Mussolini, nine million Italians from the south emigrated to the north in search of jobs. By 1970, with the rapid economic recovery nearly complete, Italians started to stay put in their newly prosperous country. Now immigrants, particularly those from Italy's struggling former colonies in Africa and Albania, began to view Italy as a desirable destination. With the demise of the Soviet Union and communism in the early 1990s, Italy became a transit country for many from former Soviet Satellite countries—essentially a gateway for immigrants leaving the east to cross into Western Europe. Italy was perceived by immigrants to be a soft underbelly of the European Union (EU), a place with vast coastlines and lax borders that might serve as an entry point to all of Europe, since continental border controls largely dissolved after the Schengen Agreement of 1995, which gave Europeans the right to move freely between most contiguous western European countries.

Arezzo is a microcosm of this larger European phenomenon. The city is located in a regional zone of heavy industry that requires significant immigrant labor, especially in the textile industry. The comparatively new diversity among Arezzo's population is visible even to the casual observer. There are residents from Southeast Asia, China, Eastern Europe, and Africa, as well as Roma ("gypsies"). Twelve percent of Arezzo's current population are immigrants, who tend to be younger than the native-born Italian population.

An Asian clothing store.

Employees welcoming diners to Sushi Bar Number One on the Viale Michelangelo Buonarroti.

Immigrants also have higher birthrates, which is perceived by some to be an encroachment on Italian culture. Immigrants are frequently referred to as *extra-communitari*, or non-EU citizens.

Many southeast Asians immigrate to Arezzo to work in the gold and jewelry industry. They often come to Italy as a family unit, with the men working at a jewelry factory, while young mothers in Asian dress and sandals, with small children in tow, walk in groups around the town during the day. Noticeable markets for the immigrant population in Arezzo include specialty food shops full of rice, produce, curry, and coconut, as well as a few Asian clothing stores with brightly colored women's accessories. Some southeast Asians, most often single men, sell long-stemmed roses in local restaurants, while others roast chestnuts on autumn nights on Corso Italia. These immigrants are not independent entrepreneurs, but are indebted to a modern version of a local *padrone*, or godfather, from their home country who helped them immigrate to Italy, and to whom they must pay back their travel expenses. Undocumented immigrants are sometimes little more than disenfranchised wage slaves. It is an odd echo of the experience Italian immigrants had a century before.

Chinese immigration to Italy is relatively new, but it is increasing at a rapid pace. Many Chinese immigrants come to Italy as expert tailors, working within the textile industry in the Valdarno region, using their sewing skills to turn out merchandise for the global fashion and apparel markets. Others arrive in Italy without documentation, accepting menial jobs as custodians and cleaners to save money to send to their families in China. Still others run small businesses in high-profile locations, such as a popular pizza shop on Corso Italia. There are a handful of Chinese restaurants located behind the Arezzo train station, and down Via Petrarca there are scores of small Chinese businesses. The Aretine press frequently runs stories about Chinese immigrants, often expressing discontent about their lack of assimilation into Italian culture.

Eastern Europeans from Romania and Albania have become the new *golondrine* (seasonal workers) in Italy. Almost always women, and frequently from the same family, they provide eldercare to Italy's aging population. Because they are from an EU-member nation, they do not need a visa to enter Italy and can work legally. They fit in more easily than Southeast Asian or Chinese immigrants, who must struggle to stay in the country legally and who face larger cultural hurdles of language and customs. For example, Romanians are predominantly Christian, speak a Romance language, and are able to travel home more frequently and at a far more affordable cost than immigrants from farther away. They are able to retain a regional identity, in spite of the fact that Italians are always quick to remind eastern Europeans of their geographic origin.

Café de Tanger is one of many kebab shops in Arezzo.

Samura, from Nigeria, sells tissues, umbrellas, and other items to passersby in Arezzo's historic center.

African immigrants come to Italy through a variety of channels. Many still arrive by boat via the island of Lampedusa off the coast of Sicily. They come from francophone countries such as Morocco, Algeria, and Tunisia, along with sub-Saharan countries like Chad, the Democratic Republic of the Congo, and Senegal. Fluency in French makes for an easier language transition to Italian. Many African immigrants walk up and down Corso Italia and through the historic center of town, selling small items for cash like tissues, cleaning rags, or umbrellas. Single African women are also more common compared to other immigrant groups in Arezzo, and some are street vendors along with many of the men. Sadly, many African women have been human-trafficked into the sex trade and stand alone or in pairs next to busy roads outside of town.

The Roma are also a presence in Arezzo and are recognizable by the women's long braids and skirts. Occasionally they are costumed in surprising attire such as whiteface and tattered gowns in order to attract the attention needed to beg successfully for money. The gypsies often move from town to town, according to the public market schedule. The Roma are a stateless people who refuse to be documented by authorities. They are culturally conservative and deeply clan-conscious, living together in makeshift camps and communities at the outskirts of towns. Their origins are disputed, but research indicates that they migrated together in one group from northwestern India to Europe around a thousand years ago. The presence of Roma is an ongoing issue throughout Europe and receives a fair amount of public attention—most of it negative and rooted in fear and folk legends about kidnapping children and stealing.

The community of Arezzo addresses the needs of documented and undocumented immigrants through local nonprofit organizations such as Migrantes ONLUS and Cooperativa Beta. These non-governmental organizations (NGOs) work to ease the transition to Italian culture for immigrants and provide support for families. Public sentiment toward immigrants in recent years has become more negative as the immigrant populations have increased and struggled to assimilate. The Italian Parliament has passed significant anti-immigrant legislation, and public services throughout Italy have seen funding cuts. Meanwhile, the presence of greater numbers of immigrants has caused Italians to question or defend their idea of what it means to be Italian. For example, Mario Balotelli, a well-known Italian soccer player on the national team, was born in Palermo to Ghanaian parents and was later adopted by an Italian family, obtaining Italian citizenship when he turned eighteen. He is routinely heckled or taunted with shouts such as, "There is no such thing as a black Italian!" Speaking fluent Italian alone does not guarantee acceptance, and the situation has led some naturalized Italian citizens to ask, "What does it mean to be Italian or to look Italian?" Does it require centuries of family history in the same small town—perhaps a family farm, olive grove, or vineyard in the hills? Does "looking Italian" mandate a classical *bella figura* (beautiful image)? Is it a collection of received ideas about government, culture, food, and family, or perhaps a combination of all of these things?

Italy is still learning how to accept and assimilate *extracomunitari* from North Africa, eastern Europe, and elsewhere, facing the new challenges that come with trying to accommodate waves of immigrants arriving in hope of a better life. As Europe's indigenous population ages and has fewer children, Italy, with its long coastlines and proximity to Africa and Eastern Europe, will continue to be on the front line of the immigration challenge for Europe.

An example of the first musical notation, invented by Guido d'Arezzo or Guido Monaco (Guido the Monk) in the eleventh century.

Part III Culture

Guido Monaco, also known as Guido of Arezzo, Italian musicologist and monk. Painting by Antonio Maria Crespi, called *il Bustino* (1580–1630), oil on canvas, 60 cm x 51 cm (Inv. 1353). Copyright Veneranda Biblioteca Ambrosiana. (Photo by DEA / VENERANDA BIBLIOTECA AMBROSIANA / De Agostini / Getty Images)

9

Arezzo's Rich Music History

Ken Stephenson

The eleventh-century Benedictine monks attached to the old Duomo in Arezzo filled their days with the crystalline beauty of Gregorian chant. These monks chanted melodies every day as part of the detailed liturgy of the Mass and the seven daily prayer services they performed, repeating some chants weekly and others only annually. The Aretine monks sang thousands of these ethereal songs, passed down faithfully from generation to generation, most likely through oral tradition, although possibly through hand-copied books of sacred songs, perhaps with dots and squiggles marked above the words as vague reminders of the dips and turns in the melodies. But no monastery had any reliable means of recording and preserving the precise details of their chants other than institutional memory—that is, until Guido Monaco came along.

Guido is one of the most influential teachers in music history. His two seminal innovations—staff notation and sight-singing by syllables—continue to be used by teachers, students, composers, and performers a millennium after their introduction to a handful of monks in Tuscany. Staff notation had existed earlier in some form, and also underwent important later refinements, but Guido made the musical modernizations workable and set them on the path to universal acceptance. He invented the means to encode musical sounds onto paper as well as decode that notation back into sound. Guido's contributions increased the speed of learning music, provided for the document-based preservation of musical compositions, and facilitated the transmission of new music, especially at great distances.

Mounted above a window on the west side of Arezzo on the Via Cesalpino just north of Via Montetini, a stone plaque commemorates one of the supposed birthplaces of Guido Monaco (Guido the Monk). We do not know his exact place of birth, but a few details of his life survive through his musical treatises and one preserved letter. The designer of the Arezzo memorial accurately portrayed Guido's two primary innovations. First is the standard medieval staff of four lines: one fewer than the five lines of standard modern notation. Musicians had experimented with notating melodies using long horizontal lines prior to the eleventh century. These lines originally represented harp strings, one line per pitch, and each syllable of the sung text was written above the appropriate line. The horizontal line arrangement proved impractical for any but the simplest melodies, since most songs employ eight or nine different pitches, and a typical human cannot scan nine parallel lines for long without getting lost or dizzy. Guido's ingenious solution was to use both the lines and the spaces between them, placing the text underneath the staff and marking the corresponding pitches with marks on the staff. While

Guido's memorial plaque on the house in which he was born.

today's note heads are oval, the medieval notation appeared just as displayed on the stone plaque on the Via Cesalpino. In fact, Benedictine monks still occasionally use the slightly curvy rectangles that are easy to produce with wide-nibbed pens, to notate a Gregorian chant.

At the left end of the staff is a clef, another of Guido's inventions. Without a clef to establish a place, the lines do not clearly signify anything. The bottom line, for instance, could conceivably stand for any pitch the scribe found suitable. The clef on the commemorative plaque is a stylized F (with a down stroke on the left and two little shapes to the right representing the letter's two horizontal lines), indicating that the third line from the bottom stands for the pitch F. The space below it stands for E, the one above it G, and so on.

If you remember how Sister Maria taught the von Trapp children how to sing in *The Sound of Music*, then you know how Guido arrived at his sight-singing method. Rodgers and Hammerstein simply translated Guido's idea into contemporary musical style. Examining a certain hymn for the feast day of Saint John the Baptist, Guido noticed that the opening pitches of the song's six phrases were each one step higher than the last, forming a six-note scale: C, D, E, F, G, and A. The first syllables of these Latin phrases were *ut*, *re*, *mi*, *fa*, *sol*, and *la*. Understanding the power of associative memory, Guido reasoned that a person practicing the hymn and learning to link these six syllables with their respective pitches would become familiar enough with the sound of the scale to be able to sing any notated melody. All the singer would have to do is voice the appropriate syllable, and the inner workings of the mind would come up with the correct pitch. The memorial plaque shows Guido's six-note scale—the hexachord—with their syllables going both up and down. This memorial demonstrates Guido's remarkable gift to the world.

History's greatest music teacher welcomes all visitors who arrive in Arezzo by train. When they come out the front door of the *ferroviaria* and look straight up Via Guido Monaco to Piazza Guido Monaco, they will see the statue of the musical monk. A closer look shows him holding a book with musical notation on its pages, the gracious Benedictine perpetually offering his useful creation to all posterity. The bronze relief sculpture on the east side of the pedestal of the statue suggests why Guido invented his methods. He is teaching a choir with several men standing in the back row and a young boy in front. (The Italian word *soprano* has a masculine ending because of the all-male choirs of this era.) Every young man coming to the monastery, whether to take his religious vows or just to learn to read, also had to learn to sing. There were thousands of Gregorian chants to learn, with some repeated only very rarely. It likely took half a lifetime to memorize the melodies. Guido, ever the practical teacher, wanted to find a better, quicker, surer way to learn songs than rote drill. His two methods revolutionized the study of music. Because of him, anyone—anywhere in the world—who was well trained in the techniques of staff notation could sing by syllables and perform a new song perfectly without ever having heard it before.

The new methods worked extremely well, and many of the older brothers resented Guido's success. Guido's opponents ousted him from his monastery, but a friend, Bishop Theodaldus of Arezzo, gave Guido a job teaching choirboys at a cathedral located outside the Arezzo city wall, just southwest of the present-day train station and close to the campus of the University of Siena at Arezzo.

Close-up of the Guido Monaco statue.

A statue honoring Guido Monaco in the center of a piazza that also bears his name is located near Arezzo's train station.

Relief on the Guido Monaco statue.

Fortunately for the history of music, Pope John XIX heard of the controversy surrounding the musical monk and invited Guido to Rome to demonstrate his new methods. Claiming to have taught the Pope to sight-sing in three days, Guido received full exoneration and reinstatement. Whether we owe our musical system to the Pope's fortuitously good ear or to his teacher's wily diplomatic skills, we may never know.

Arezzo Pop

In more recent years, Arezzo has become a focal point for Italian pop music. Almost every summer since 1987 (with nearby Sesto taking over the duties a few times), Arezzo has hosted the Arezzo Wave Love Festival, which showcases Italian pop and rock artists on several stages for four or five days each July. The program usually features a few performers from other countries, as well. American acts Sonic Youth, David Byrne, and Moby have all participated in the festival. Over the years, Arezzo Wave has branched out to incorporate world music, comedy, and other related performance arts. The 2012 event included music by Tibetan Buddhist monks, a break-dance contest, and a tribute to John Belushi.

One of the acts that has performed at Arezzo Wave is the local alternative rock band Negrita.

Seward (Spagna) performed on the Main Stage at the Arezzo Wave Love Festival in 2014. (Photo provided by Arezzo Wave)

Negrita is an Italian rock band from Arezzo. (Photo by Roberto Serra—Iguana Press / Getty Images)

Front man and Arezzo native Paolo "Pau" Bruni sings in a low register similar to that of English-language rock stars like Brad Roberts of the Crash Test Dummies, with a touch of the gravel of an Alex Band (The Calling) or Eddie Vedder (Pearl Jam). The band's powerful, moving lyrics exhibit a prominent streak of world-weariness. The lyrics of "Rumore," for instance, include noises from the television that pound the brain like a steam train. "Lontani dal Mondo," about two friends sitting in a car at night talking about how strange life is, includes in its lyrics the imagery of two raindrops sliding down the window, seemingly unaware of each other. "Ho imparato a sognare" offers a ray of existential hope—friends come and go, the song observes, but when you realize you are just standing around in your underwear, everything starts to look better. Negrita's sound began with the guitar-driven textures of hard blues, alternative rock, and grunge. The group began experimenting in recent years with other sounds: electronics, reggae, and even—in the song "Gioia Infinita," for instance—the happy trumpets and parallel thirds of Mexican mariachi.

As a result of the efforts of the Jazz Club Arezzo and other Italian enthusiasts of the great American art form, Arezzo also hosts a summer jazz festival. Usually held in either the Anfiteatro Romano or the nearby Arena Eden, a movie theater built into the southern angle of the medieval wall, the annual event offers three to five days of Italian jazz combos, ranging in size from quartets and quintets to large swing bands. Recent years have offered tributes to John Coltrane, Stevie Wonder, and Django Reinhardt.

The Festival Cameristico Internazionale has brought world-class classical chamber music to Arezzo every spring since 2006. In recent years, the concerts have taken place right in the center of old Arezzo, at the Casa Museo Ivan Bruschi at Corso Italia 14. At the half-dozen concerts each season, some of the best musicians in the world perform powerful music by the master composers of the eighteenth, nineteenth, and twentieth centuries. The 2011 Festival Cameristico included a performance by Ingolf Wunder, the 2010 winner of the Chopin Competition, and in 2012 Haochen Zhang, the 2009 winner of the Van Cliburn Competition, played at the festival.

But any exploration of the music of Arezzo must include several visits to the Duomo. Many public services include music, and local music teachers sometimes hold their studio recitals there. The sonic beauty of the church bells that peal out regularly across the city further add to Arezzo's musical soul.

An advertisement for a music event at La Basilica di San Francesco.

La Pieve di Santa Maria in Piazza Grande.

10

Film in Arezzo

Ralph Beliveau

These stories may seem familiar:

—Two lovers are torn from each other on their wedding day when the woman suffers a fatal snake bite. The man steals his way into Hell to get her, but since he loves her too much, he cannot trust that she is following him out of Hell. He looks back, she fades, and he is stuck with his uncontrolled passions.

—A rich man pretends to be two other people so a girl will love him. An older doctor wants her for himself. The girl is mad because of the deception, and agrees to marry the doctor. When the imposter reveals who he really is to the girl, she marries the rich man.

—A man falls in love with a younger girl and tries to leave his wife and kids to be with her. The wife considers killing the kids, but eventually decides on a murder-suicide pact with her husband.

—A very strong man (who is actually the son of a god) is hired by a king to teach his sons. But the king gained his throne by killing his own brother. The strong man falls in love with the king's daughter, but when he goes after the treasure the king stole from his brother, the king tries to kill him. The man eventually defeats the king, then leaves with the deceased king's daughter.

—A man marries the girl of his dreams, but their town is taken over by an invading army. The invaders put the man, his wife, and her son in a place where they will be killed. The man tries to help his son stay calm by pretending their imprisonment is a game.

These plot summaries cover a wide range of Italian culture. The first three are Monteverdi's *L'Orfeo*, Rossini's *The Barber of Seville*, and Bellini's *Norma*, respectively. In the fourth, the very strong man is *Hercules* from the 1958 Italian film directed by Pietro Francisci. And the last is the plot of *Life Is Beautiful* (*La Vita è Bella*), the 1997 international box office smash written and directed by and starring Roberto Benigni. These five movies are worth considering together because of what they tell us about Italy. The plots contrast the basest of human desires and actions with the highest of culture's aspirations. This contrast makes Italian film compelling, whether one considers the experimental daring of neorealism in the 1940s and 1950s, the art films of the 1950s and 1960s, the exploitation films of the 1970s and 1980s, or more recent movies.

Motion picture poster for the film *Cabiria*

Many Italian films find their meaning through a sense of the place, whether the focus is on the whole of Italian culture or the regional sensibilities of Tuscany or Arezzo. Often, the reach of high culture and the plunge into low culture are seen as simultaneous parts of the same moment. Italian film has had a history of combining epic themes with popular tales to attract large audiences.

A Silent-Era Historical Epic

Early twentieth-century Italian silent cinema caused ripples that reached all the way to Hollywood. In 1914, Giovanni Pastrone made *Cabiria*, a three-hour historical epic that featured elaborate, detailed sets, enormous crowds of cheaply paid extras, and a creative team obsessed with historical accuracy. The film told the story of the epic battle between heroic Rome and evil Carthage, accompanied by the love story of a Roman spy who saves the slave girl Cabiria from sacrificial death to the Carthaginian god Moloch. A loyal slave named Maciste, who became an important fictional character in Italian film over the next fifty years, assisted the spy in the daring rescue.

Cabiria was popular in Italy because it told a familiar historical story on a scale that was simultaneously spectacular and melodramatic. These characteristics carried over to Hollywood when the film was screened in the United States. The American cinema pioneer D. W. Griffith was impressed by the possibilities of the historical epic. *Cabiria* influenced Griffith's work on *Intolerance* (1916), which weaved four historical epic strands together around melodramatic plot elements. Hollywood's early tradition of epic historical filmmaking was inspired by Pastrone's example.

Mysteries

American author James M. Cain published his popular mystery novel, *The Postman Always Rings Twice*, in 1934. It's a quick, hard-hitting story of a woman who works in a roadside restaurant with her husband. They hire a drifter to help out in the diner, but the wife secretly becomes the new employee's lover, and the two plot to murder her husband. After they kill the husband, it isn't long before the couple turns on each other. Visconti released an Italian film version of the story in 1943 called *Ossessione*. However, Mussolini's Fascist government quickly suppressed and destroyed the film due to the influence of American popular culture and the general sordidness of the storyline. Luckily, Visconti had hidden away a second negative of the film.

Neorealism

Ossessione is often cited as the first Italian neorealist film. The neorealist subgenre would become one of Italy's great international exports, as Visconti, along with renowned directors such as Roberto Rossellini, Vittorio De Sica, and Federico Fellini (at least in his early work, before he veered into the fantasy genre) attracted the praise of critics around the world. De Sica's 1948 film *Bicycle Thieves* (*Ladri di biciclette*) is considered by many critics to be one of the best films ever made. But this critical praise did not translate into universal box office success in Italy.

Art Films and Comedies

Federico Fellini moved away from Italian neorealism and grew to be one of the main proponents of a different kind of sensibility in Italian film. Where neorealism offered audiences slice-of-life real worlds, some filmmakers sought to expand into fantasy. Examples include: Fellini's *La Dolce Vita* (1960) and *8½* (1963), Michelangelo Antonioni's modernist anxiety tales *L'Avventura* (1960), *Eclipse* (1962), and *Blow Up* (1966), and Pier Paolo Pasolini's examination of sexual mores in *Mamma Roma* (1962) and *Il Decameron* (1971). Other directors brought a broad comic sensibility to film, including Pietro Germi's 1961 *Divorzio all'Italiana* (*Divorce Italian Style*).

The 1950s and 1960s also saw several Italian actors gain international acclaim. Sophia Loren, who won an Academy Award in 1961 for her work in Vittorio De Sica's 1961 *La Ciociara* (*Two Women*), became synonymous with 1960s Italian glamor and style. Other Italian performers who commanded the world's attention included Vittorio Gassman, Marcello Mastroianni, Ugo Tognazzi, Claudia Cardinale, Gina Lollobrigida, and Nino Manfredi. At the same time, Italian films often used American and British actors as leads to help encourage international distribution.

Sword-and-Sandal Movies

One popular genre of Italian movies of the 1950s combined elements of historical epics and Hollywood B-picture cinema. This new genre of historical costume dramas was called *peplum*, or "sword-and-sandal" films. Producers sensed that classical, mythological Rome was familiar enough to draw Italian audiences, but could also be exploited for international crowds.

A good example of this genre is the 1958 version of *Hercules* (*Le fatiche di Ercole* / *The Labors of Hercules*), directed by Pietro Francisci and starring the American body builder Steve Reeves. The realism of historical epics was replaced by fantasy elements from classical mythology, along with a love story that emphasized the sexuality of a damsel in distress. *Hercules* was an enormous international financial success. In the end, approximately three hundred sword-and-sandal films were made, spawning a subgenre that influenced American films such as *Jason and the Argonauts* in 1963, *Clash of the Titans* in 1981 (remade in 2010), and *Gladiator* in 2000.

Horror and Western Films

Hollywood's growing influence spawned two other genres of Italian films: "spaghetti horror" and "spaghetti westerns." Made in Italy, these films often chronicled stories of the old American West and were filled with blood and violence.

Scholars of Italian cinema have only found one horror title produced before 1956: *The Frankenstein Monster* (*Il Mostro di Frankenstein*, 1920). The production of horror films was more or less banned during the Fascist era as they were seen by officials as decadent and the government-controlled film industry did not finance horror and fantasy stories. Instead, depictions of social realist films and light escapist comedies (called "white telephone" films) gained favor between 1922 and 1946, leaving no internal tradition of horror cinema on which to build. In 1956, however, filmmaker Ricardo Freda directed a landmark film, *I Vampiri*. Freda completed only half the film, and his cinematographer Mario Bava finished the remainder. Bava became an innovator in early Italian horror movies and is particularly known for the 1960 film *Black Sunday* (*La maschera del demonio*), which chronicled the story of a vampire-witch who was executed by her brother.

These early horror films soon gave way to more naturalistic murder mysteries that came to be known as *giallo*, or "yellow," in reference to the color of the paperback murder thrillers put out by the Italian publishing house Mondadori. The yellow films proliferated from the 1960s to the 1980s, and typically featured striking set design and photography, as well as women menaced by darkly clad shadowy figures ready to mete out brutal violence. This form's most highly regarded director is Dario Argento, who made films like *The Cat o' Nine Tails* (*Il gatto a nove code*, 1971) and *Deep Red* (*Profundo rosso*, 1975).

Over three hundred "spaghetti western" films were made between 1963 and 1969. The best known were directed by Sergio Leone and starred Clint Eastwood, and include *Fistful of Dollars* (1964), *For a Few Dollars More* (1965), and *The Good, the Bad and the Ugly* (1966). As with the peplum, an American star helped in marketing the films. Eastwood's portrayal of the antihero "The Man with No Name" would set the tone for hundreds of Italian-made westerns to follow. The films were frequently shot in Spain, replaced Indians with Mexicans, introduced romantic subplots, and used exaggerated violent imagery. The strength of their imagery influences cinema to this day, with current American directors like Quentin Tarantino and Robert Rodriguez bringing the genre back into vogue. Tarantino pays homage to many "spaghetti" characteristics in his highly acclaimed and controversial film *Django Unchained* (2012), which is a reimagining of an Italian Western.

A Passage to Arezzo—*La Vita è Bella* and Roberto Benigni

Wandering through Arezzo, visitors see signs that proudly indicate the locations where Roberto Benigni's 1997 movie *Life Is Beautiful* (*La Vita è Bella*) was filmed. The picture won three Oscars at the 1998 Academy Awards, including Best Foreign Language Film, Best Music in an Original Dramatic Score, and a Best Actor award for Benigni, who famously climbed over the Los Angeles illuminati at the ceremony to receive his award from fellow Italian Sophia Loren. Benigni was born only a stone's throw from Arezzo, and the first part of his film features not only the city, but also the local countryside. As Benigni, who plays the movie's lead character, Guido, says to a friend in Arezzo's Piazza Grande, "I tell you! We're in a city! We can do anything we want. You want to let yourself yell. . . . yell!"

The film contains a strong populist sentiment. For one, it is grounded in the physical comedy of its star/writer/director Roberto Benigni. Benigni's physicality recalls the great works of Charlie Chaplin, Buster Keaton, and especially Harpo Marx. American director Jim Jarmusch, who worked with Benigni in *Down by Law* (1986), *Night On Earth* (1991), and *Coffee and Cigarettes* (2003), said of Benigni in a 1992 interview in the *New York Times*:

> It would be easy to label Roberto as being some kind of insane mixture of Buster Keaton, Toto and Harpo Marx. But the truth is that Roberto is truly unique. Like Harpo he does have an amazing anarchistic quality. He can walk into a room and turn it upside down or make it explode. His true gift is improvisation and, I would add, disruption. Working with him is really a riot because you don't know what to expect from him.

The comparison to Totò is apt, since that Italian comic actor, who appeared in ninety-seven films between 1937 and 1968, also ventured into poetry and screenwriting toward the end of his career. Benigni, on the other hand, got his start in a kind of poetry that was specific to rural Tuscany: the *poeti a braccio*. This kind of street poetry, grounded in complex improvisational uses of rhyme schemes, contrasts with the physicality—the pratfalls, the bumbling, the comic misidentifications and mistakes, the lurching satire of goose-stepping—that he employs in *La Vita è Bella*.

Benigni sets the first half of *La Vita è Bella* on the streets of Arezzo, which would have been the largest town near the area where he was born, in the rural countryside of Manciano la Misericordia, just outside of the small walled city of Castiglion Fiorentino, between Arezzo and Cortona. Coming from modest means, Benigni's father moved the family to Prato, just north of Florence, when Benigni was six years old.

Growing up in Prato, Benigni learned of Dante from his father, and of Arezzo's native poet Petrarch. But it was in improvisational poetry that Benigni found his true artistic muse. The form requires a sophisticated understanding of meter. In a 2001 interview with Carlo Celli, Benigni explained:

> In Tuscany and upper Lazio, the ancient region of Etruria, there remains a complex tradition of alternating rhyme schemes of the octet as used by Ariosto and Berni. These rhyming couplets are tremendously hard to grasp, among the most difficult in the world. I always tell poets to begin from the octet because if one can master the octet then everything else comes easily . . . the rhymes are alternating and closed, but in the improvised octet they never close.

This complex understanding of the way improvised poetry can be performed aspires, like an opera, to high art. At the same time, its improvisational character aligns with Benigni's physical comedy and reflects the way humor and surprise are interrelated, using a clever phrase constructed in the moment to create a sudden turn or fall that completely reverses our expectations of what may happen next.

Reversal is at the center of *La Vita è Bella*. The film earnestly contrasts the love story of the first act, set in Arezzo's timeless walled cityscape, with

The locations of La Vita è Bella "then and now."

the tragic inhumanity of a German concentration camp in the second act. However, Guido's positive spirit resists the temptation to get dragged into the tragedy that surrounds him and his family. He decides to create a fantasy for his son, in order to make the misery more endurable.

This is a hard turn to make, and the film certainly had its share of detractors who felt that the two worlds were unbridgeable. For some viewers, the stark contrast between the story line and the realities of the Holocaust is troubling. For others, the film provides a creative context for exploring the human need for art and humor. Some critics of *Life Is Beautiful* have questioned Benigni's sources for the film. His father, whose experiences inspired the film, was not Jewish, but was instead drafted into the Italian Fascist army that occupied Albania.

Another way of understanding the film is to view it as a realist fable trying to balance the tensions of the true and the mythical. Benigni imagines Arezzo as an ideal place, a representation of the fairytale of old Europe that still survived in the twentieth century. Guido is portrayed as a clown without the trappings of face paint and an exaggerated form. He lives, instead, in the space just beyond the normal boundaries of acceptable human behavior.

Another route to understanding the polarities in the film (spoiler alert) comes with the realization that the story is framed by voiceovers from Guido's son, Giosue, at the beginning and end of the film. Giosue thus becomes the "author" of what we see. Clearly Giosue's version is tied to what he learns from his mother and father (just as some of the story is constructed from Benigni's father's recollections). Giosue is telling the story from the point of view of a middle-aged man recounting what he learned as a boy. In the voiceover at the beginning, Giosue says, "This is a simple story but not an easy one to tell. Like a fable, there is sorrow, and, like a fable, it is full of wonder and happiness."

The translation of *favola* as "fable," however, might be better thought of as "folktale." "Folktale" fits better with the magical side of the story, especially the idyllic Arezzo setting and the heroic central character. The Arezzo of Benigni's film is a place where accidents, coincidences, and chance meetings are part of daily life. Guido adapts—just as his personality will later and more tragically in the concentration camp. It is useful to understand the film both as a fable and as a folktale, both as a historical account and as a personal memoir shared between father and son. It is clear that Roberto Benigni returned to his earliest childhood memories of Arezzo to connect to the way the child character, Giosue, would see the world in the first part of the story.

Benigni's tragicomedy exemplifies the same radical combinations that one finds throughout the history of Italian cinema. A comedy about a concentration camp is not so far from fake spaghetti Westerns, or films marrying high classical culture with strongman morality tales. A key to understanding Italian film is recognizing the contrasts contained in cinema, both dedicated high art and mass entertainment. Benigni's *La Vita è Bella* is a gateway to the exploration of Italian film more generally. By traveling among different genres, across different historical periods, the viewer can develop a deep and wide appreciation for using film as a way to come to understand a culture—especially in Italy.

La bella figura (literally "the beautiful figure") is a way of life in Italy that governs style, behavior, and the idea that one must always make a good impression.

11

Elegance and Fashion in Arezzo

Ryan Bowling

Sunglasses, shoes, catwalks in Milan, and trend-setting fashion houses with famous family names—there is no brand with so much ubiquitous appeal as "Made in Italy." As part of the peninsula's diverse but exquisite fashion, Arezzo makes a unique contribution to Italy's timeless style.

Style in Italy has been reborn in recent years and channeled through a Renaissance expression of personal savoir faire known as *sprezzatura*. Like much of Italy's fashion history, sprezzatura is a quirky manifestation of personal fashion. It draws its origins from the classic Italian text *The Book of the Courtier* by Baldassare Castiglione. Castiglione was the definition of a Renaissance man and was likely writing about himself and his very fashionable contemporaries when he defined sprezzatura as "a certain nonchalance, so as to conceal all art and make whatever one does or says appear to be without effort and almost without any thought about it." Visitors to Arezzo may view a certain nonchalance and easy elegance in the city's most fashionable citizens. In reality, however, the Arezzo style is both studied and well thought out. Sprezzatura is often described as having the appearance of "studied carelessness." However, it is precisely this "studied carelessness" that remains hidden to many admirers around the world. Arezzo and its well-dressed denizens may hold the key to better understanding what it means to have Italian fashion and style.

Take an afternoon walk around Arezzo's city center and you won't get far before the small medieval city's glamorous style grabs you by the collar. Perhaps inspired by their heritage of famous artists and frescoes, grand piazzas, and

Scarves and ties at Banchelli on Corso Italia.

even grander wealth as a center of the Italian gold trade, the Aretines are as well dressed as any of their big-city visitors.

Most of the city's shopping can be found along Corso Italia in the center of town. The Corso, as it is often called, is not unlike the winding historical road by a similar name in Rome—the Via del Corso. As with Rome's famous street, Arezzo's Corso is a cultural and social conduit for the city's residents and visitors alike. It is located near many of the city's main artistic, architectural, and cultural destinations. The Corso is truly representative of the city's ancient past and promising modern future.

The retailers who call the fashionable Corso home include bakers providing fresh bread for the family meal and small grocers with local cured sausages and seasonal vegetables. The frequent lines at the *gelateria* are constant reminders that food and fashion happily coexist in Arezzo, with locals and visitors alike cooling off and shading themselves from the sun in Italian-made sunglasses from Ray-Ban, Persol, or Prada. Dotting the avenue are purveyors of housewares and home

Menswear that is "Made in Italy" at Banchelli.

The high fashion retail store Sugar on Corso Italia.

furnishings, treasured antiques, and heirloom jewelry, as well as international fashion and clothing retailers like Foot Locker, United Colors of Benetton of Treviso, and Italy's own Victoria's Secret–like brand, Intimissimi. Tucked in between the trendy international chain stores are some true style makers, the men and women who curate and craft the city's enduring modern personal aesthetic.

At the leading edge of Arezzo's city center, at Corso Italia 279, is Banchelli. Just across the Via Spinello from the train station, Banchelli is one of the oldest and most influential clothiers and fashion makers in Arezzo. A men's-only store with expertly tailored, luxurious clothing from world-renowned Tuscan and Umbrian clothiers like Brunello Cucinelli and Boglioli, it also carries luxury lines from across the country like Etro and Herno. The store has two well-appointed floors welcoming shoppers to touch, feel, and try on the latest fashion and style from across Italy. Expect skilled advice from the well-dressed and attentive staff, as they subtly pass along the art of studied carelessness in creating your own personal style. Whether it manifests itself through a simple change in shoelaces, using your necktie as a pocket square, or rolling the left sleeve of your sports coat to reveal a monogrammed shirt cuff and a vintage watch, Banchelli teaches how to be a local *con stile* (with style). Banchelli promises in its store and on its website to promote "fashion that is recognized in the discretion of refined elegance and never performed," which is a good modern definition of sprezzatura.

Continuing up the Corso, one finds the most provocative and originally decorated storefront in the city. The large-paned windows and their creative contents belong to the high-fashion retailer Sugar.

Two storefronts, known respectively as "Donna" (Woman) and "Uomo" (Man), face each other from either side of the Corso and contain fashion fresh off the runways of Milan, Paris, and New York. Like Bergdorf-Goodman in New York, Neiman Marcus in Dallas, or Collete in Paris, Sugar plays a significant role in shaping its city's fashion and style. As Banchelli does for men, Sugar provides a highly stylized experience for its female clientele, with clothing from the world's most sought after fashion labels like Burberry, Comme des Garçons, and Helmut Lang, as well as well-known "Made in Italy" labels like Dolce

The window presentation in Alessandra's shirt store on the Via de' Redi.

Alessandra Ligi is well known for her custom-tailored shirts.

& Gabbana, Gucci, and local fashion superstar Prada. Sugar has become a regional fashion destination and a modern interpretation of the classic Italian clothier, offering personalized service that helps to sculpt the individual style of its patrons.

While Sugar focuses on bringing high fashion to Arezzo from runways around the world, and Banchelli offers artisanal fashion from nearby tailor houses turned global clothiers, the quintessential style maker of Arezzo is a true sartorialist who can craft one of the most essential items in any wardrobe, the perfect shirt. Alessandra Ligi and her eponymous store is hidden just off Corso Italia on the Via de' Redi. Buried among the endless bolts of fine cotton, countless needles, spools of thread in every color, and disheveled stacks of custom shirt patterns, Alessandra has a warm smile and bright eyes. Her store is chaotic, but the disorder is honest. Alessandra, who will frantically dig her way out of the reams of fabric to greet you personally, runs her store and hand-tailors the shirts on her own. She is one of the most influential style makers in Arezzo.

The studied carelessness that Baldassare wrote about centuries ago can be learned best in Alessandra's shirt-making shop. Do you want a spread collar or a straight collar? Is this a casual shirt or a formal one? Would you like the Italian-length tails or the American? Do you prefer buttoned or French cuffs? These are the classic Alessandra questions that make her store a classroom and a laboratory of Italian fashion. She comes by her craft as a tailor through trial and error, as well as hard work. Time with Alessandra is time well spent, and it results in a great custom-made shirt.

Alessandra's story is quintessentially Italian. She began sewing under the watchful eyes of a local artisan, who also happened to be her neighbor, when she was eighteen years old. She learned to craft clothes through basic templates for a shirt or a pair of pants. In her family of artisans, she learned to sew with precision and speed. Most importantly, she learned the enduring art of personal style that she calls "classic chic." She came to believe that, while fashion often fades, personal style can live on forever. It is this sentiment that inspired her, after a thirteen-year apprenticeship, to open her own store in Arezzo in August 1994. Alessandra found a small space outside the center of town where she filled thirty square meters with her passion for precision and creation. After five years, Alessandra's business outgrew its modest home, so she returned to the center of Arezzo, just off the Corso, where at the age of sixteen she once sold sports apparel. From Arezzo's city hall to Piazza Grande, one can see Alessandra's "classic chic" everywhere.

Even the well-tailored men and women at Banchelli and Sugar trust Alessandra's talent, guidance, and the learned carelessness that her store inspires. Her influence has not stopped at the edge of town, but as it has grown she has remained humble and determined to make a shirt "as good as your own skin." As she thought about her life and her work, she recently wrote:

> Rispetto al mondo della moda Italiana io sono il classico granello di sabbia nel deserto, ma in questi anni ho conosciuto tante persone e mi rende fiera sapere che in qualche parte del mondo c'è stato, c'è o ci sarà qualche uomo che indossa un capo o un accessorio con il mio nome.
>
> (With respect to the world of Italian fashion, I am really the classic grain in the desert sands. Through the years, however, I have gotten to

know so many people and have developed a reputation in different parts of the world that there is, was, or will be some man that has an item of clothing or an accessory with my name on it.)

Whether a shirt says Gucci, Prada, Cucinelli, or Alessandra, it is clear that "Made in Italy" is one of the most desirable brands in fashion. Arezzo is a good place to glimpse why Italy plays such a large role in setting trends in world style. With all of the fashion retailers that line the city's Corso, Arezzo has become a destination and even a laboratory. Perhaps the best place to linger and take in the fashionable sights, sounds, and styles of Arezzo is just steps off the Corso in Piazza di San Francesco. Under the shade of an umbrella and in the shadow of Basilica di San Francesco, one can linger over an espresso or a glass of Tuscan wine as Arezzo's best-dressed citizens collect at the cafés that dot the small piazza. Many are there for the *aperitivo*, a tradition of late-afternoon socializing while enjoying a refreshing spritz and light local fare before the evening meal. Still others have collected in the square to catch up on the comings and goings of their neighbors and friends. There is no shortage of ideas, opinions, or friendly gestures. Arezzo is a community of individuals with an easy elegant style to match. On any day of the week, a traveler here may sit in a piazza among Italy's merriest, and most fashionable, people.

The "studied carelessness" of sprezzatura highlights the way many Italians dress and cary themselves in public.

Nineteenth-century cookbook with shopping lists.

12

Aretine Food and Culture

Donna Logan

The culture of Tuscany has stimulated the imagination of world travelers for centuries. Since the grand tours of the nineteenth century, travelers have come to Tuscany from every corner of the globe with the intent of paying homage to the art of the Renaissance and the gentle countryside. Lurking in the back of every traveler's mind is always the anticipated delight of savoring the celebrated Italian cuisine.

An authentic Italian eating experience, however, can be challenging to discover. Understanding and making the most of a Tuscan meal takes some cultural mediation. Aretines take great pleasure in the foods of their region and are decidedly proud of the perfect balance they have achieved in serving and preserving typical dishes from long-but-not-lost traditions. How does one understand and navigate the regionally specific cuisine of Arezzo?

Soup of the Day—Etruscan, Roman, or Tuscan

Arezzo has been an important economic center for over three thousand years. Walking around the city center, one finds remains of Etruscan and Roman walls, streets, squares, and sculpture interspersed with medieval and Renaissance buildings. The evidence of these enduring cultures makes for a daunting amount of historical fallout to sift through, especially when it comes to food. A traveler or student arriving in Italy soon perceives a striking truth—Italians have serious and typically rigid ideas about when and how to eat. Change is not easily embraced. Take this rule up a notch when talking Tuscan food. Basics

This hearty bean soup is served at Ristorante Il Cantuccio located on the Via Madonna del Prato.

that were popular in ancient times are still enjoyed today. Typical dishes made with *farro* (spelt, a type of wheat), which is used in numerous salads in the summer and delightful rosemary-infused bean soups in winter, have been common since the time of the Etruscans. Other legumes, the most popular being the *cannellini* white bean and several varieties of *ceci*, or chickpeas, continue to be enjoyed in traditional as well as updated recipes. These ingredients were plentiful during both Etruscan and Roman times and enjoyed by all social classes. Fruits and vegetables were common, as were roasted and grilled meats. Archaeological finds attest to the extensive use of olive oil as a foodstuff, a salve for wounds, and even as a cosmetic in Roman times. Moreover, the abundance of spectacular vineyards throughout Tuscany, thanks to a perfect combination of soil, terrain, and climate, have made wine the drink of choice, with evidence of its consumption dating back as far as the eighth century B.C.E. After three millennia, it is no wonder locals have well-defined opinions of the proper way to prepare, serve, and enjoy these foods.

For an Italian there is an appropriate time to drink an espresso as opposed to a cappuccino, to have lunch and dinner, and to serve bread at the perfect moment during a meal. Parmesan cheese is not to be served with just any pasta dish, and ice is not to be served in just any drink. This may be baffling to a visitor and leave them perplexed, but these mores are based on century upon century of tradition.

The Legacy

For centuries, after the fall of the Roman Empire, Arezzo had a quiet, mostly agricultural, economy. Landowners and farmers made up the local aristocracy. Because the city was not located on a major route of transit, the food culture was far less influenced by foreign travelers than by habits imported from other parts of Tuscany. Hence, the area was accustomed to reaping and enjoying the fruits provided by the local land.

Even though the distance between Florence and Arezzo is less than an hour by train, there are major differences between the people and the cuisine of the two cities. The Aretines have been defined, since the time of Dante, by their rather rough means of expression and level of communication. They tend to be direct and entirely convinced that their methods of food preparation are the best.

The Aretine table is straightforward and characterized by simple preparations of absolutely top-quality ingredients. The fertile hills and atmospheric conditions of the area make for excellent grapes, mostly Sangiovese, which variety serves as the basis for extraordinary local Chianti and other wines. Extensive olive groves, characteristic of the Tuscan landscape, produce spectacular oil. Raised only in this area is the special Chianina breed of cattle from which the famous Florentine *bistecca* is prepared. There are other local specialties that include particularly tasty potatoes and beans from the Casentino area, as well as several outstanding sheep's milk cheeses from throughout the region. Local herbs include rosemary, sage, wild fennel, and a particularly small-leafed variety of mint (*nipitella*), all of which blend together harmoniously to make for a perfect peasant or aristocratic meal.

Italians enjoy a frothy cup of cappuccino in the morning.

Crostini, an appetizer of small toasted bread slices that can be topped with meats, vegetables, cheeses, herbs, or oil.

Antipasto means "before the meal" and is the traditional first course of a formal Italian meal.

A meal in Arezzo is a celebration. Whatever event is being commemorated—a birthday, a holiday, the last day of school, or the opening of a store—inevitably the party will begin with mixed crostini. Traditionally, these small toasts come in two varieties—red and black. The red crostini consist of a smooth, spicy tomato mixture on top of toasted bread. The black are topped with a coarsely ground rustic chicken liver pâté served with capers, often a bit of anchovy, and frequently a splash of *vin santo* to add smoothness. (Vin santo, which translates as "holy wine," is a sweet, after-dinner, portlike wine.) Other seasonal crostini toppings include white cannellini beans seasoned with generous oil, salt and pepper, slow-cooked kale in a light tomato sauce, or a mushroom sauté. Depending on the season, these crostini may be complemented with *bruschetta* (be sure to pronounce this word correctly, with a hard "k" sound for the "ch"), served with a rub of garlic and extra-virgin olive oil, or some chopped fresh tomatoes seasoned with salt, pepper, basil, and oil. Frequently crostini are served together with or followed by an array of typical cured meats—prosciutto *crudo*, Tuscan salami, and *finocchiona*. The local prosciutto tends to be a tad more flavorful than its northern cousins, but not as salty as the southern versions. Tuscan salami is veined with lard and speckled with whole black peppercorns to make for a well-balanced cured blend. Finocchiona, also referred to as *sbricciolona*, is a tender, uniformly ground salami that is generously flavored with fennel seeds.

After the antipasto (which is eaten before beginning the real meal) comes the first course of local pastas. For a special occasion, this would usually consist of a homemade egg pasta, plain or filled. Variations include *tagliatelle* or *pappardelle* (flat egg noodles that are named according to the width of the cut), or ravioli filled with egg and spinach. If you're from Casentino, the ravioli will be filled with potato. These pastas are all served with a ground meat and tomato sauce. It is a slow-cooked delight that pairs well with grated parmigiano cheese. A variation of the theme might be the "naked" ravioli, known locally as *ignudi*. These special ravioli are an egg, ricotta, and spinach mixture cooked as small dumplings (no pasta sheath), served with a sage-infused melted butter and parmesan sauce. It is surprisingly light and, perhaps not surprisingly, delicious.

The main course is usually made up of mixed grilled or roasted meats. These include the exquisite Chianina steak or *tagliata*, served with warmed olive oil aromatized with generous amounts of rosemary, garlic, black pepper, and

Pasta with truffles.

salt. The main meal can also include chicken, sausages, ribs and, on occasion, game such as rabbit. The sides include white beans, potatoes and, when in season, a bit of tender salad.

Dessert is simple, although the traditional Aretine treats have given way to more decadent sweets prepared in the local *pasticcerie*. Given the tradition of outstanding pastry chefs in Italy, homemade desserts are basic and few. These include the most popular *crostata*, a sweet-crust tart filled with fruit jam or, at its best, a fig and walnut compote. Several pastry shops in town provide an array of small pastries. There is also always the tender-crusted traditional cream and pine nut "Torta della Nonna" (Grandmother's Cake), and the ever-popular *cantucci*—crisp, almond-filled, twice-baked *biscotti* cookies. These are made to be dipped into a small glass of Vin Santo to end the meal.

A Word About the Bread

Throughout the centuries, bread has held a pole position in Aretine cuisine, even though the local version has long been an undistinguished white-flour loaf. The subpar Aretine bread is a historical anomaly, due in large part to the Florentine domination of Arezzo in the 1500s. Florence placed a huge tax on salt, and the Aretines decided to rebel against their rulers by baking saltless bread. Over the many decades of Florentine rule, the local population grew fond of the taste of the somewhat flavorless bread. Although it does goes well with famous local savory cured meats and salamis, it is nothing to write home about.

Tuscan olive oils have a robust flavor with a peppery finish.

Piadine, a flatbread sandwich with a variety of fillings, is an example of Italian fast food.

Traditionally, bread was baked in the community oven, but neighborhood bakeries and modern-day kitchens have democratized the cooking of this staple good. Bread used to be a precious commodity and baked just once a week. It was eaten not only as a side at meals, but also for breakfast with homemade jams and marmalades or as a snack with olive oil or a slice of ham. At special meals, the bread was served with a multitude of toppings, and once it began to age, became the basic ingredient for *panzanella*, a delightful bread, tomato, red onion, cucumber, and basil salad in the summer. Other uses for stale bread include *pappa al pomodoro*, a thick bread-based tomato porridge, and *ribollita*, a magnificent vegetable and bread soup eaten in the colder months. Aretines never let bread go to waste, and these traditional recipes continue in the local diet.

Back to the Future

As in all other parts of the developed world, the daily diet in Arezzo and throughout Italy is changing in response to a multitude of modern nutritional needs and time constraints. Nowadays, it is rare to have someone at home tending to slow-cooked meals and long lunchtime rituals. Today's students often have just a short break at lunch, as do professionals working in office jobs. Modernity has mandated the option for a quick and satisfying meal, and there are several choices around town. These meals range from a

This gastronomia is located inside Eurospar Santa Prisca, a grocery store in the city center.

very basic sandwich, *panino*, to a slice of pizza, from a quick dish of freshly prepared pasta to a kebab. Other varieties of Italian fast food include a very local version of a hamburger and fries, and sausage or roast pork sandwiches. Another option is an expressly made *piadine* (a flatbread "baked" when ordered), filled with grilled vegetables, soft cheeses, and cured meats. Finely prepared food can also be purchased in the many delicatessens located across town and the surprisingly well-supplied *gastronomia* located within Arezzo's supermarkets. Even a chain grocery store like the local Despar will have well-informed professionals who willingly advise on the numerous choices of prosciutto, pecorino cheese, and other delicacies.

Quick meals are also available at both large and small coffee bars or cafés. Frequently, one will find an array of satisfying salads, cooked vegetables, and small sandwiches from which to choose.

A Word on Gelato

It would be remiss to not say a word or two about *gelato* as part of Arezzo's gastronomic offerings. Gelato is going for the gold internationally in recent years, giving ice cream a run for its money as a top dessert. *Gelaterie* sell artisan-made ice cream all over Arezzo. Some of the best gelato in Italy can be found inside the old city walls. There are traditional flavors such as rich chocolate, hazelnut, and vanilla, but also exotic walnut,

Gelato is a creamy frozen Italian treat with a growing international popularity that rivals ice cream.

Food trucks at Arezzo's Saturday market sell cured meats and cheeses.

almond, chestnut, or pine nut, fruit ices and creams, fig and ricotta, gluten-free, lactose-free, or yogurt-based organic varieties throughout town.

Buon Appetito!

After centuries of cherished traditions, there is an almost physiological need to understand and further develop the art of Italian cooking. Aretines are excellent interpreters of beloved standards—ribollita, pappa al pomodoro, and roasted and cured meats. Professionally trained young Italian and foreign chefs are also creating food that is delightful to both the eye and the palate at restaurants throughout the city. What was once considered a "poor" kitchen in Italy may at times appear extravagant to a foreigner. Consider the magnificent porcini mushrooms gathered in the Casentino hills, either fried or grilled, in the autumn; or a special variety of artichoke found in early spring that is eaten raw with other locally produced vegetables, *pinzimonio* style. These were once peasant foods that are now gracing the tables of the world's finest restaurants.

Whatever your budget, time restrictions, or venue of choice, an essential element to enjoying Aretine cuisine, and Italian food in general, is to stop and allow your senses to savor what you are eating. The Italian saying *non si invecchia a tavola* literally translates to "one does not age while sitting at the table." Long lunches and longer dinners are a way of life. Even the aperitivo, with its multitude of tapas-like snacks, is a festive, celebratory act. It is true that Italians never tire of eating, but they also ceaselessly talk about food, planning dinner at lunch and reminiscing about breakfast at teatime. The Italian and Aretine passion for food is unending. Food nourishes not only the body, but also the soul. Take your time, enjoy, and eat with your friends and family. It is an irresistible part of Aretine life.

Polenta with mushrooms.

Italian desserts come in many shapes, sizes, and colors.

Tuscanative sells wine produced in Tuscany as well as other parts of Italy.

13

The Wine of Tuscany's Arezzo

Susannah Gold

Wine has been part of Arezzo's history for centuries. The Greeks were the first to bring the vine to Italy, including the Valdichiana—the valley in and around Arezzo, which at the time was primarily known for growing cereals. Amphorae, the double-handled narrow-necked jars, that have been discovered in Italy confirm that grape growing and wine making in the Valdichiana dates back to the seventh century B.C.E. These jugs were used to transport wines on sea voyages and over land throughout Italy and beyond. Interestingly, wines made in amphorae have come back into vogue in recent times. According to some Italian producers, amphorae are the perfect vessels for aging wines.

Population growth around Arezzo in the fifth century B.C.E. meant that vine growing became more diffuse. Arezzo developed into a well-regarded area for the production of pottery used for wine throughout the Mediterranean, and remained so into the second century A.D. In those times, wine was drunk only by the noble classes or to celebrate religious rites. Generally, wine was diluted with water before imbibing. Drinking undiluted wine was thought to be uncouth, something that barbarians did. Early Italian wine was sweet and aromatic, while most of the wines produced today are dry.

It was not until the fifteenth century that Arezzo's wines were judged for their quality. An official registry indicated that wines from the Valdarno di Sopra (hill) were considered to be of superior quality, while the wines from around the piano di Arezzo (valley) sold for a lesser price. In the seventeenth and eighteenth centuries, Tuscan agriculture began to change from cereal to wine production. The wines from the Valdarno di Sopra were considered to be premium regional wines. In fact, Cosimo III de' Medici in 1716 announced a "Bando" designating four areas for quality wine production—Chianti, Pomino, Carmignano, and Valdarno di Sopra.

While the Arezzo area is one of the lesser-known wine regions within Tuscany today, in the eighteenth century it was among the most famous. Tuscan wines are usually some combination of Sangiovese and other grapes. Sangiovese is the principal grape variety in Tuscany and much of Central Italy. Other grapes that are generally used in wines in the Arezzo area include both indigenous varietals and international grapes. Some of the most common native grapes are Canaiolo, Ciliegiolo, Malvasia Nera, Trebbiano Toscano, Malvasia Bianca, and Grechetto. International varieties also do very well in the soil around Arezzo, and numerous varieties are grown, including Cabernet Sauvignon, Merlot, and Syrah for red wines and Chardonnay for white wines.

Local wine and cheese pairings highlight regional cuisine.

The area can be separated into four main wine-growing regions: Casentino, Valdarno (right bank), Valdarno (left bank), and the Valdichiana. Italian wines are generally classified into a pyramid of quality with the highest designation being the *denominazione d'origine controllata e garantita* (DOCG), followed by the slightly lesser *denominazione d'origine controllata* (DOC). In the province of Arezzo, only one wine has the highest quality rating: the Chianti Colli Aretini DOCG. With new European Union rules designed to create some unification among nations producing wine, DOC and DOCG are now also known as *denominazione di origine protetta* (DOP) wines.

Outside of Arezzo are slopes and plateaus with acres of beautifully tended vines. The trellising systems in the area make for a uniform and glorious landscape. The Etruscans settled here long ago, and the fields have been cultivated ever since. The centuries of labor and care make for manicured and orderly fields. Gorgeous drives lined with cypress trees often lead up to the main house of the vineyard. Italians and foreigners alike fall in love with the beautiful rustic country houses surrounded by vines.

While many grapes grow in Tuscany, Sangiovese is king. Sangiovese expresses different aromas and flavors depending on the soil it grows in, the microclimate where it flourishes, the exposure of the grapes to the sun, the altitude of the wineries, the direction that the slopes face, and many other factors that are generally packaged together and called terroir. The wines made from in and around the Arezzo area are predominantly Sangiovese-based wines.

Sangiovese generally produces wines that are a light ruby red color, with medium body and very good acidity. A wine with good acidity pairs very well with food, offsetting and enhancing the meal while not overpowering it. When tasting a wine made with Sangiovese, don't be surprised if it has more acidity than a California Cabernet Sauvignon. It's supposed to be bolder because it must pair with the local cuisine of charcuterie, cheese, pasta, tomato, and meat dishes such as *finocchiona* and *capocollo*.

There are good and bad vintages for wine, and this is particularly true in the subregions. Generally, however, what changes from year to year is the quantity of grapes that are harvested, rather than the quality. The growing season is long, and much can happen in the vineyards during the course of the season. However, thanks to careful viticulture practices, there will always be a harvest. The year 2003 was hot throughout the spring, summer, and fall, and as a result that vintage will not age well. Aging is also known as cellaring or laying down. In order to be cellared, wines must have enough structure to withstand aging. Hot years like 2003 produce wines that are bigger, fruitier, and more alcoholic, but with less acidity and thus less of a chance of aging well. Some wines are only good to drink once they have been aged for a long period of time; others are better closer to the year of the grape harvest.

Agro-tourism allows visitors to get a glimpse of rural Italian life. La Striscia, just outside Arezzo, is a working farm and winery that also accomodates overnight guests.

Many have heard of the famous "Super-Tuscan" wines such as Tignanello or Sassicaia. A "Super-Tuscan," a term not often used anymore, is a wine made from a blend of Sangiovese and international grapes such as Cabernet Sauvignon or Merlot, or from international grapes alone. The Super-Tuscans were very much in demand from the 1970s to the 1990s. These blends have declined some in popularity as people return to the indigenous varieties, but the Super-Tuscans are still among the top Italian wines in the world. One very famous Super-Tuscan comes from the Arezzo area and hails from a winery called Sette Ponti, owned by the Moretti family. Their wine is called Crognolo and is approximately 90 percent Sangiovese and 10 percent Merlot. The Moretti family winery was at one time the property of His Royal Highness, the Count of Torino, Vittorio Emmanuele di Savoia, the son of Umberto II, the last king of Italy before Italy became a republic. The Moretti family bought it in the 1950s. Another very famous winery in the area that also makes a well-known Super-Tuscan is Il Borro. Owned by the famous Florentine family Ferragamo, their wine is made from a blend of 50 percent Merlot, 40 percent Cabernet Sauvignon, and 10 percent Syrah. The winery dates from the 1700s, when it was a property of the Medici family.

Cellared wine at La Striscia farm and winery.

Proximity to water and mountains has an impact on grape growing and wine making. In the Tuscan region, it is the Arno River and the Pratomagno Mountain range to the east. When a vineyard is close to a water source, it usually has fertile soil. It also tends to be humid and somewhat warmer than at high altitudes. Depending on the grape variety and the desired style of wine, this can be a positive or a negative factor. It is positive if you want your grapes to have "noble rot" (Botrytis Cinerea) so they will wither on the vine, creating a great dessert wine such as Sauternes. It is considered a negative if you want to make a very dry wine from a grape variety that suffers from diseases. Mountains tend to shield a vineyard from harsh winds and create a microclimate that is generally warmer and more favorable to the vine. It is said that great wines are made in the vineyard rather than in the cellar.

Generally speaking, areas that have a long growing season with diurnal temperature changes (warm days and cool nights) produce grapes with sufficient ripeness in their tannins and other positive elements. These grapes are then made into wines that tend to have structure as well as balanced aromas and flavors. Higher altitude vineyards often produce wines with good acidity, which can be essential to both the longevity of the wine and its ability to pair well with a variety of foods.

Chianti Colli Aretini DOCG is one of seven subzones of Chianti. Many indigenous varieties grow in this region, and some are being resuscitated after almost going extinct. A number of

Terra Bianca vineyards in the hills outside Arezzo. (Photo by Charles Kenney)

Quench is a local wine shop located on the Via Ristoro D'Arezzo.

wineries are growing quasi-extinct varieties of grapes such as Foglia Tondo, Barsaglina, and Pugnitello. All of these grapes tend to be converted into single varieties instead of being used in blends. Even the international varieties that grow in these soils are a little different than when grown elsewhere. The Merlot is a little leaner, and the Cabernet Sauvignon tends to have more restrained fruit than the same wines from Chile or Argentina. A number of wineries are also practicing organic or sustainable viticulture, including a cooperative called Paterna Società Agricola Cooperativa and the winery Mannucci Droandi.

While the Chianti Colli Aretini DOCG are perhaps the most widely known of Arezzo's wines, the Valdichiana DOC also have a rich history. The area is famous for its agriculture, including grains and cattle. It is also now home to a host of grape varieties that grow well both in its hills and its valleys. One area winery, Fattoria Santa

Vittoria, actually has an experimental section in which grape varieties are tested to see what can grow well in the region. The winemaker at Santa Vittoria is a handsome young man who fell in love with the owners' daughter. He proudly shows the small plants he grew in the experimental part of the winery. His pride and joy is the Pugnitello grape, which he and a handful of other producers are trying to bring back and sell. Pugnitello is a charming wine with aromas of spice and black fruits and a little bit of pepper.

Another area to watch is the Cortona DOC just fourteen miles (22.5 km) south of Arezzo. Most Americans know the Cortona area as the setting of Frances Mayes's best seller, *Under the Tuscan Sun*. This area is slowly making a comeback among connoisseurs of wine. In the past twenty years it has become widely known for its Syrah, one of the few areas in Italy where Syrah grows well. The Syrah grown here is big and powerful with a lot of pepper and spicy notes. Cortona's hot, dry climate and sandy soils are exactly what Syrah requires to show its best face. One of the top wineries in the area is Tenimenti d'Alessandro, which makes a number of well-known wines from Syrah. Another DOC in the area is called Pietraviva DOC. Pietraviva wines are made largely from either Sangiovese for reds or Trebbiano for whites.

Along with Sangiovese, the red wines may contain Canaiolo and Ciliegiolo, two classic Tuscan varieties. Malvasia Bianca best exemplifies the single-variety whites. Malvasia is a white grape that produces wines that tend to have good fruity and floral aromas on the nose and flavors on the palate. It is generally delicate and can be cultivated either into a sweet version or a dry one. Pietraviva DOC also allows for the use of "international" grapes such as Cabernet Sauvignon, Chardonnay, and Merlot, in addition to the more traditional, indigenous varieties.

Not all producers in the Arezzo area use the DOC denomination. Some Aretine winemakers use an alternative denomination called *Indicazione Geografica Tipica* (IGT) because it gives them more freedom in how to make their product, including which techniques and grape varieties to use in production. While this is a lower denomination on the quality pyramid, these wines can be extremely expensive and are very well known.

In Arezzo's city center, the association Strada del Vino Terre di Arezzo plans tourist visits to local wineries. The Strada del Vino is a winding road through local Arezzo vineyards that extends for approximately two hundred kilometers.

Tuscan wines are usually some combination of Sangiovese and other grapes.

Strada del Vino Terre di Arezzo helps tourists plan visits to local wineries.

It passes through the Chianti Colli Aretini DOCG, Valdichiana DOC, Cortona DOC, and Pietraviva DOC. Along the way, visitors can try the dry and sweet wines and taste the local foods that pair so beautifully with these wines.

Almost all of the winemakers that you will meet if you tour the Strade del Vino Terre di Arezzo will tell you about their soils, microclimates, and grape varieties. Many will talk about their wines as if they were talking about their children. It is a pleasure to behold how attached they are to their beautiful vineyards, giving them the same care and love as centuries of Tuscans before them.

Wine has been a part of Arezzo's history for centuries and is an important part of any meal.

Piazza Grande during the Saracen joust that takes place twice a year in June and Steptember. (Photo by Shelby Stillwell)

14

The Medieval Joust

Gina London

Amid colorful costumes, vivid twirling flags, and triumphant music, Arezzo's spectacular jousting tournament takes place every June and September in the Piazza Grande of the town's historic center. The joust symbolizes Arezzo like nothing else. Adjectives like "resplendent," "dazzling," and "magnificent" describe La Giostra del Saracino, or the Joust of the Saracen. The pageantry begins with the ominous sound of drums in the distance followed by a blast of trumpets joining the beat. Then come the boisterous marching men in procession, walking in precise formation up and down the streets in bright outfits. Some wave and throw decorated flags, others beat the rhythmic drums hanging from their necks or blow fanfares on stretched-out medieval-looking trumpets. The participants wear tights, short black boots, and long colorful tunics that flare out at the end.

The events began in the Middle Ages when the knights of the Crusades dashed off to vanquish the "Infidels" or "Saracens," common terms used by Europeans to define Muslims and other non-Christians. The reenactments in Arezzo were contests for sport and not war. First recorded on August 6, 1535, Arezzo's jousting tournaments were held throughout the sixteenth and seventeenth centuries and then more sporadically during the eighteenth and nineteenth centuries. Since 1931, however, the competitions have again become regular biennial events. The first joust is held on a Saturday in June and is officially known as the Joust of San Donato, commemorating Arezzo's patron saint.

According to tradition, Saint Donato performed a miracle by successfully serving communion from a broken glass chalice after the heathens shattered it.

But then in 362 B.C.E. he was decapitated in Arezzo under the rule of the pagan Roman Emperor Julian for his Christian faith. His body is said to be interred in Arezzo's Duomo, but the Church of Santa Maria, just down the hill from the Duomo, claims his head, encased in a golden, jeweled bust-shaped shrine.

The second joust tournament is held on the first Sunday in September during daylight hours. This late-summer joust is named for the Madonna del Conforto, in honor of another of Arezzo's patron saints. The Madonna is actually a relief of the Virgin Mary on a small glazed terracotta plaque. In 1796 when Arezzo was besieged by a series of earthquakes, a group of faithful knelt in a wine cellar to pray. The relief of the Virgin was hanging nearby on the basement wall. Legend says that as the people prayed for the earth to stop shaking, the Madonna suddenly glowed bright white and the tremors stopped. The Madonna del Conforto is featured in her own chapel in the Duomo, and every February 15th a festival is held in memory of her earthquake-ending miracle.

The Chimera is a mythical fire-breathing beast that serves as a mascot of Arezzo's Porta del Foro neighborhood during the joust.

The joust is serious business to Aretines, and they go all out to cheer for their teams to win the competition. The tournament revolves around four teams corresponding with the four main doorways of the old walled city. These four divisions represent real rivalries stemming from medieval times when the town was basically quartered into four independent villages through towered enclaves protected by armed guards.

Today's joust teams draw their district boundaries from these historic neighborhoods and are referred to in Italian as *quartieri*. In addition to quartieri museums, the districts also have clubhouses and public squares set aside for special meetings, dinners, and recreation. Like passionate American college football fans, Arezzo's residents are proud of their neighborhood identity. Each section flies its quartiere flags and displays its colors on stores and *palazzo* buildings. The *Porta Crucifera* (Door of the Cross) neighborhood boasts banners in red and green with an emblem of three hills and the Church of Santa Maria. The Porta Sant'Andrea (Door of Saint Andrew) flies flags of green and white with a silver cross in the center. The Porta Santo Spirito (Door of the Holy Spirit) is represented with yellow and blue flags with a large dove in the middle. The Porta del Foro (Door of the Forum) rests under fuchsia and yellow banners with a startling chimera monster in the center.

The chimera, the mythical fire-breathing lion with the head of a goat on its back and a snake for a tail (chronicled in Allison Palmer's chapter on Arezzo's art and art history), is also a symbol for the entire city of Arezzo. Children's sports teams have chimeras as mascots, and the city's community swimming pool and gymnasium complex is

The marching men of La Giostra del Saracino. (Photo by Mary Margaret Mason)

named for the beast. The chimera holds special pride for the Porta del Foro quartiere because an ancient Etruscan statue of a chimera was excavated near the neighborhood's gate. Considered one of the most famous pieces of Etruscan art, the bronze original is in the Archaeological Museum in Florence. A copy of the chimera stands guard inside Porta del Foro's arched doorway.

During the joust, the four neighborhood teams compete fiercely for the best scores so that they can claim bragging rights to the coveted *Lancia d'Oro*, or Golden Lance, given to the winning section of the city. Although it may be called a lance of "gold," the lancia is actually carved in wood specially for each joust. The city holds a design contest, and local artisans compete to carve the winning concept. Over the years, the elaborate designs have included serpents, angels, and even a pope. Each neighborhood team has its own Giostra del Saracino museum that displays its array of golden lances.

During the Giostra, it is easy to join in the spirit of the event even if you are not a local. Vendors set up tables on the streets, selling flags and scarves, bracelets, necklaces, whistles, and even miniature drums emblazoned with a team's colors. There is an air of excitement in Arezzo in the weeks leading up to the joust. The four neighborhoods hold dances at night, and children are invited to participate in pony rides complete with miniature jousting lances. Team practices are held in Piazza Grande and are free and open to the public.

Without a doubt, however, the most raucous pre-tournament events are the dinners each quarter hosts throughout the week before the joust. Families, friends, team captains, and the honorary knights attend these communal feasts. After purchasing a ticket, the diner will be invited to take a seat with the participants at one of the many long tables set up alfresco in the center of the district. Typical meals include pasta, grilled meats, and plenty of wine. Singing, dancing, and general merrymaking often last until dawn, although the knights are always sent to bed early to get a good night's sleep before the big event.

On the morning of the joust, a reverberating blast of cannon fire resounds throughout the town center at seven o'clock to signal the start of the tournament day. The next cannon salute comes four hours later at the Piazza della Libertà, in front of Arezzo's town hall. The town herald unfurls a scroll from the building's second-story window and dramatically reads the "Proclamation of the Joust." The knights and representatives stand below, festooned in regal attire in the colors of each quartiere, holding an assortment of crest-covered banners. Musicians and flag wavers, along with a phalanx of armed men clasping large metal spears, also stand at attention. This ornate procession winds its way through almost all of the main streets in the center of town, ensuring that no one misses the splendor.

Later in the afternoon another cannon blast signals the Blessing of the Knights. Priests arrive in each neighborhood square to bestow prayers on the team's knights and their horses. Then another procession brings the four teams together at the city's Duomo where they are all blessed again—this time by the Bishop of Arezzo—accompanied by another sounding of the cannon. By evening, the Piazza Grande is transformed into a boisterous jousting arena surrounded by high-rise bleachers. Spectators pack the square facing the long dirt track, or *lizza*, that stretches from one end of the piazza to the other. The fifth cannon salute triggers the opening ceremonies. The drum and bugle corps play while each team's captain rides on horseback into the arena wearing an elaborate helmet and flanked by a costumed entourage. The music continues as skilled flag throwers, known as *sbandieratori*, present a performance to the assembled crowd.

Arezzo's sbandieratori are part of an independent organization of flag wavers, drummers, and trumpeters. They tour and perform across the world. Their colorful costume and flag designs depict the coats of arms of each of the thirty-nine municipalities in the province of Arezzo and are inspired by the paintings of the fifteenth-century early-Renaissance artist Piero della Francesca. The Arezzo flag throwers association is proud that all of its flags are still handwoven and hand-painted to maintain authenticity.

The flag wavers' elaborate displays were originally used as communication devices to convey movements and strategies to allied warriors. Performances now include precise choreography and accuracy as members hurl flags high in the air to their partners and then acrobatically flip over their flags and each other. During the Giostra pre-show, two sbandieratori will square off in an impressive theatrical flag battle called "the skirmish" that symbolizes the struggle between good and evil.

After the intense warmup, the knights take center stage. Each neighborhood puts forward two men who take turns riding a horse, at full gallop,

Joust pageantry and celebrations.

Flag bearers proudly wave their colors.

The joust mannequin: The Saracen.

pointing their lances toward the enormous Saracen mannequin known as "Buratto, King of the Indies." Buratto is carved of wood and mounted on a swiveling post. Wound up tightly and holding three leather balls hanging from chains in his outstretched right hand, Buratto grips the score shield in his other hand. Before each run, two hulking guards insert a target sheet onto Buratto's shield. A red cross divides the paper with a bull's-eye in the center. Each quadrant of the sheet, including the cross lines, is worth varying numbers of points. The red bull's-eye is worth the most at five points.

The knights charge toward the shield and the bull's-eye in a dramatic and dangerous display of accuracy and dexterity. They must race to the score shield while aiming for the center. At the same time, each jouster must take care to avoid being walloped by Buratto's menacing weapons, which could result in the loss of two points. If the charge is deemed too slow, the knight could also lose two points. All points are deducted if the rider falls from his horse. If the shock of the blow to the shield breaks the lance, the knight is awarded double points. The tournament's scoring system is complex.

As soon as each knight completes the charge, the guards rip down the score sheet and take it over to the jury balcony, composed of a group of Aretine judges, who determine the number of points to be awarded. The lance is darkened at the tip, much like chalking a pool cue, so that

Joust items on display at the Palazzo della Provincia.

A knight charging Buratto. (Photo by Devon Kysor)

it imprints onto the score sheet. It can make for time-consuming and excruciating deliberations. While fans yell their own interpretations of the run, the judges agree on their decision and hand down a folded slip of paper to a courier, who walks it over to the herald, who makes the formal pronouncement of the score to the anxious crowd. When the final charge is completed and the winning quartiere is announced, a raucous cheer erupts from the crowd. A final series of cannon blasts combine with the shouts of joy from the victors and the jeers from neighborhood rivals.

The celebrations after the event often spread from Piazza Grande to Corso Italia and up and down other smaller streets as euphoric Aretines wave their flags and scarves. Some climb their way up to the Duomo, where they jubilantly congratulate the arriving victorious team and their horses as they appear on the cathedral's steps. The large wooden doors of the church are opened wide, and the winners stride in, accompanied by the triumphant march from the Italian opera *Aida*. There are tears, hugs, and high-fives as the knights and their associates make their way to the front of the nave. The Golden Lance is laid in front of the altar, where the team kneels in prayers of thanks. Based in medieval history and folklore, Arezzo's modern-day Giostra del Saracino is filled with all the pomp, circumstance, and revelry of a different time. In the modern world it creates a strange and powerful bridge between generations and eras.

Conclusion

Suzette Grillot & Rebecca Cruise

For those fortunate enough to have lived and worked in Italy, returning is always a cherished and memorable experience. There is something inviting, warm, and welcoming about this beautiful and fascinating country, which has captured the imagination of millions of visitors. There are few experiences in life greater than staring up at Michelangelo's Sistine Chapel, tasting that first bite of fresh *ragu* sauce after a long absence from the country, or sitting in an outdoor Italian café sipping a glass of expertly aged Chianti while taking in the surroundings. It is no wonder that the country has captured the hearts of so many of its guests.

Tuscany, in particular, has enchanted generations of travelers—and Arezzo is no exception. From its hilly cobblestone streets and lively piazzas to the colorful views of vineyards and olive groves, Arezzo is one of many jewels in the crown of a region that has become synonymous around the globe for the good life. To study or vacation in Tuscany is to enjoy life's rich pageant of food, art, music, history, and culture. Yet Arezzo remains a relative unknown to foreign visitors. Wishing to share a small piece of this lovely Tuscan town, its people and its history, *Buon Giorno, Arezzo* is a reflection of the personal experiences and expertise of a number of contributors who have had the great pleasure of getting to know this city on a hill that overlooks the Valdarno—or the Valley of the Arno River.

(*facing*) Arezzo is a real Italian city in the heart of Tuscany. Off the main tourist path it maintains a population of about 100,000 people.

The volume you have just explored provides a brief but illustrative overview of the various aspects of life in this lovely city. It highlights a fascinating political, artistic, and linguistic history, offering a sampling of the intrigues and

Plants and flowers adorn doorways in the historic center of Arezzo, making ordinary entrances extraordinary.

contributions of the city and its residents. Contributors also examine the challenges of the current geographic and demographic realities in Arezzo. And finally, they tempt us with wonderful descriptions of the sights and tastes of Tuscany and Arezzo—food, wine, fashion, and film—arguably some of the greatest culture in the world.

This book is intended largely for students and travelers alike, but anyone interested in Italy will enjoy each slice of daily life described in its pages. Arezzo is a magical, but also very real, city, and we hope to have introduced readers to the nuances that make it such a special place. Although not all facets of Arezzo have been examined, the book gives the reader a sense of the city's history, people, and culture—and hopefully whets the appetite for more.

The story of Arezzo demonstrates the typical experience of rise, fall, and regeneration. For its more than two thousand years of history, this town has drawn people in due to its natural resources and ideal location. Arezzo developed as a religious center during the Roman era and rose to prominence in the eleventh century. Its growth and expansion were impressive. Florentine domination, however, had a significant impact on the Arezzo's vitality and strength, eclipsing the city's political, economic, and social development throughout the Renaissance—a period when Italy came into its own.

Arezzo, and Italy more generally, has also faced change in more recent times. In the last century and a half, far-flung provinces and towns up and down the peninsula were united into a modern state. Even after Giuseppe Mazzini and Giuseppe Garibaldi brought the nation together, crushing rural poverty and the hope of seeking a better life in faraway lands led to significant emigration out of the country throughout the late nineteenth and early twentieth centuries. Ironically, some of these

An aedicula, or small shrine, to Santa Maria.

Ristorante Il Cantuccio on Via Madonna del Prato.

The Dini family butcher shop on Via Madonna del Prato.

same factors make Italy attractive to immigrants today.

In between, Italians fought two world wars on their own soil. Arezzo still bears the distant marks of these difficult times. World War II, in particular, took a toll on Tuscany as the Nazis retreated from the oncoming Allied forces, often leaving a scorched earth in their wake.

As several authors mention, the wounds of the last century, along with a long tradition of provincial attitudes, have constrained the development of a strong national identity. The challenge remains similar to what the Italian nationalist Massimo d'Azeglio said a century and a half ago, "We have made Italy. Now we must make Italians." However, the cohesive identity that Italy lacks at the national level thrives when it gets closer to the people—at its most local. With a strong sense of belonging to the communities in which they were born and raised, Italian cities like Arezzo possess unique bonds among its longtime residents. It is still the exceptional Aretines (or Italians from other communities, for that matter) that stray too far from home for too long. Aretines may be friendly, outgoing, and warm to foreigners in their midst, but the deep bonds of school groups that are developed early in life make social integration for outsiders a difficult prospect. Such bonds and the strong sense of local belonging, however, inspire visitors, and many Aretines stay closely rooted to families and friends, remembering from where they came.

Figure on top of the Soprintendenza building.

Despite barriers to assimilation, foreigners flock to Arezzo. Immigrants from Africa, Eastern Europe, Western Europe, China, and the United States add to the color and diversity of the city. This new and exciting multiculturalism enhances the city's local flavor. Visitors to Arezzo can enjoy it all—music, film, fashion, food, or wine. The true Italian experience can be had by lounging in Piazza San Francesco after lingering over a long dinner with friends. On a daily basis, residents and visitors gather to eat gelato and take a passeggiata slowly up and down Corso Italia, admiring the effortless and unique style of those around them. The pleasure Italians take in life is not only tradition, but is also part of who they are. It is something to behold and savor.

Detail above the doors of the Duomo.

Palazzo Perelli-Marsupini, in the center of Arezzo.

Bar Stefano on Corso Italia.

Food trucks at Arezzo's open-air Saturday Market sell locally cured meats and cheeses.

Although Aretines live what appear to be extraordinary and enjoyable lives, they too have experienced the ups and downs of the global economic downturn like the rest of Italy in recent years. But Arezzo lives on and thrives despite, and even perhaps because of, these challenges. Many citizens in Arezzo have taken up social causes and have become engaged in local and national politics in response to a gridlocked and inefficient political system in Rome. The Movimento Cinque Stelle (the Five Star Movement), which has gained national and international prominence in recent years for its efforts to combat rampant political corruption and promote environmentalism among other things, is visible in Arezzo. Other members of the community have become involved in nongovernmental organizations and other forms of community action. The national headquarters for Oxfam (an international group of seventeen organizations working to find solutions to poverty and injustice) is located in Arezzo—and the city has organizations working on issues from immigration reform and environmental protection to conflict resolution and human rights. These efforts tend to look uniquely Italian, building on their tight community and familial bonds.

Perhaps one of the greatest signs of hope in Arezzo is its youth—and in particular its college student population. Home to the University of Siena in Arezzo, the city reflects an intellectual dynamism that is critical for the future. Moreover, the presence of the University of Oklahoma in Arezzo, as well as other American university programs, such as Oberlin College and the University of Rochester, for example, contribute significantly to the city's vibrant and energetic nature. The connections being made in Arezzo between local Aretines and international students, faculty, and staff create an atmosphere of curiosity, tolerance, and mutual respect. In today's Arezzo, bonds are being built that will affect the city, the country, and their relations with others for years to come. This special relationship has obviously also positively affected the contributors to this volume and undoubtedly the thousands of international students who have made Arezzo their home for a brief time.

One cannot, therefore, be anything but optimistic about Arezzo and its future. We hope that this volume has enhanced awareness about and an interest in this lovely Tuscan town. All of us encourage you to travel to, study, and settle into Arezzo so that you too can enjoy the city's charms and become attached to its way of life, just as we have.

San Polo cemetery.

Arezzo's Duomo in the late afternoon sun.

Arezzo residents purchase produce at the outdoor market on Saturday.

Contributors

RALPH BELIVEAU is Associate Professor and Media Arts Area Head in the Gaylord College of Journalism and Mass Communication at the University of Oklahoma. He specializes in the areas of critical media literacy and learning, media criticism, film and video studies, popular culture, documentary theory production and history, and rhetorical criticism. He holds a bachelor of science in media production from Northwestern University and a Ph.D. in the rhetoric of inquiry from the University of Iowa. He has taught on the subject of Italian popular and media cultures at the University of Oklahoma in Arezzo.

RYAN BOWLING studied abroad in Arezzo and graduated with a B.A. in political science and government from the University of Oklahoma. He is a partner at Black Optical, an eyewear retailer with three locations in Oklahoma City, Tulsa, and Dallas.

REBECCA CRUISE is the Assistant Dean of the College of International Studies at the University of Oklahoma, as well as Assistant Professor in the Department of International and Area Studies. Dr. Cruise specializes in security studies and comparative politics focusing on security community development, international organizations, post-conflict resolution, political participation, and gender. Her bachelor of arts is from the University of Portland, and she holds a Ph.D. in political science from the University of Oklahoma.

KIRK DUCLAUX serves as the on-site Director of Italian Programs at the University of Oklahoma in Arezzo. Duclaux holds an undergraduate degree in art history from the University of Cincinnati's College of Design, Art, Architecture, and Planning and a graduate degree from the Renaissance Art History Program offered by Syracuse University in Florence, Italy. Duclaux has traveled around Italy and educated people about art for years, formerly working as a guide for the American embassy in Rome and the American consulate in Florence before working with the University of Oklahoma's study abroad program in Arezzo.

SUSANNAH GOLD is the founder of Vigneto Communications, a public relations, marketing, and educational consulting firm dedicated to the food and wine industry. A former financial correspondent in Milan for the Dow Jones, she is also a certified Italian sommelier and pens the blog avvinare.com as "a way to stay connected in the United States to all things Italian after having lived in Italy for fifteen years." She earned her undergraduate degree at Colgate University and her master's degree in international affairs and economics at Johns Hopkins University.

SUZETTE GRILLOT serves as Dean of the University of Oklahoma's College of International Studies, Vice Provost for International Programs, and the William J. Crowe Jr. Chair in Geopolitics. Dean Grillot teaches on the subjects of global community, global security, international activism, and illicit trafficking. She also hosts an award-winning weekly talk show, *World Views* on KGOU radio, that highlights global topics and features outstanding international guests. In 2011–12, she spent ten months as Faculty-in-Residence at the University of Oklahoma in Arezzo.

JASON HOUSTON, Associate Professor in the University of Oklahoma's Department of Modern Languages, Literatures, and Linguistics, was a Faculty-in-Residence in Arezzo in 2012–13. He also served as the Director of Curriculum for the University of Oklahoma in Arezzo's program. His research and teaching focus on the foundation of Florentine humanism and Italian literature of the Medieval and Renaissance periods with emphasis on Dante, Boccaccio, and Petrarca. Dr. Houston's bachelor of arts in Medieval studies and Italian language and literature is from the University of Oregon. He also has a master of philosophy in Medieval studies and a Ph.D. in Italian language and literature from Yale University.

DONNA LOGAN works for the University of Rochester as the on-site Director of the Italian Studies in Tuscany Program. She was a lecturer of English language at the Facoltà di Lettere e Filosofia in Arezzo for twenty years.

GINA LONDON, a veteran award-winning correspondent for CNN, visited OU in Arezzo during spring 2014 to talk with students about the importance of branding and applying education-abroad experience during a career search. Today, Ms. London owns a consulting firm and provides communications coaching and training for business leaders of large and small companies across the world, including Egypt, Cambodia, and Indonesia.

BEATRICE MAZZI has served as Italian-language Instructor and Special Programs Coordinator at OU in Arezzo. She is currently in New York City at Columbia University working on her Ph.D. in Italian studies. Mazzi studied foreign languages and literatures at the University of Perugia and graduated with a degree in translation from the University of Turin. In 2010, she completed a second master of arts in comparative literature from University College London.

ZACH MESSITTE is the President of Ripon College in Ripon, Wisconsin. Dr. Messitte previously served as the Dean of the College of International Studies at the University of Oklahoma. He currently teaches politics and government and leads students and alumni to Rome each spring for a three-week course on Italian history, politics, culture, and language as part of Ripon's Liberal Arts in Focus program. Dr. Messitte earned a bachelor's degree in American history and Italian language from Bowdoin College. He holds a master's in international relations from Johns Hopkins University and a Ph.D. in politics from New York University.

ALLISON PALMER is Associate Professor of Art History in the School of Art and Art History at the University of Oklahoma. She holds a Ph.D. from Rutgers University and an undergraduate degree in art history from Mount Holyoke College with a concentration in Italian. Her research and teaching focus on Italian Renaissance and Baroque architecture, and she currently teaches undergraduate and graduate courses in art from the Renaissance through the eighteenth century, as well as humanities courses for the interdisciplinary program at the University of Oklahoma's College of Liberal Studies.

MONICA SHARP served as a Faculty-in-Residence for the University of Oklahoma in Arezzo in 2012–13 along with her husband, Jason Houston. She taught a course on immigration in Italy titled "Italy at the Crossroads." Sharp was the Director of International Student Services at the University of Oklahoma from 2008 to 2013. She has worked professionally in the field of immigration in the United States since 1997. Sharp has a B.A. in letters and Spanish as well as an M.A. in Spanish, both from the University of Oklahoma. She has traveled widely throughout Europe and Latin America. She is currently a Product Specialist for International Student and Scholar Services for Terra Dotta, LLC, a higher-education software company.

FEDERICO SINISCALCO teaches at the University of Siena and the University of Rochester. His academic interests and his teaching range from American studies to Italian studies, film studies, and documentary film production. He has directed and co-directed non-fictional films that deal with the critical reception of Antonio Gramsci, American direct cinema, Italian Americans, and the presence of American students in Italy. Currently he is working on a documentary about two Italian–African American brothers coming to terms with their mixed cultural heritage.

KEN STEPHENSON taught at the University of Oklahoma for twenty-five years. He was Associate Professor of Music Theory and the Kenneth and Bernardine Russell Chair of Music Theory in the University of Oklahoma's Weitzenhoffer Family College of Fine Arts. In 2012 he was appointed the Weitzenhoffer Family College of Fine Arts' Irene and Julian J. Rothbaum Presidential Professor of Excellence in Arts. Dr. Stephenson previously taught music courses at OU in Arezzo. He is now a lecturer in music theory at the University of Tennessee's School of Music. Dr. Stephenson has a Ph.D. in theory from the University of Iowa, a master of music in theory from Baylor University, and a bachelor of arts in music from the University of Missouri.

Index

References to illustrations and captions appear in italic type.